Bacon-Wrapped Chicken
and Chiles (page 166)

Moroccan Chicken Soup
(page 72)

Chocolate Berry Shooters
(page 262)

Dear Friends,

It never ceases to amaze what a handful of fresh ingredients, a few simple steps and 30 minutes can produce. You're on your way to turning out an impressive homemade meal—no takeout needed! Look here for fantastic fresh recipes to get dinner on the table in no time. You'll also find recipes for jams and pickled veggies that are great to have on hand and add that "something extra" which only homemade can do. While you'll spend only 20 minutes prepping these yummy additions, it takes additional inactive time until they're ready to eat—but well worth the wait!

From salads to skillet meals to dessert, it's clear that less can be more. Eye-opening Breakfast Panini (page 58), Bacon-Wrapped Chicken and Chiles (page 166) and flavor-packed Blueberry Margarita Ice Cream (page 266) are tasty examples of how a recipe can easily become more than the sum of its parts.

Whether it's your local farmers' market for interesting new ingredients like purple cauliflower (page 101), a roadside stand for freshly picked produce or your favorite grocery store committed to carrying locally sourced meats, it's worth buying fresh, in season and close to home. That's the crux of fast from scratch. Because when you start with amazing ingredients, the end result is always a fantastic dish.

So take a peek inside. We'll introduce you to new food ideas and show you how to combine fresh ingredients to make meals you can be proud of and that your family will ask for again and again—perfect for any night of the week.

Happy Cooking!

Betty Crocker

CONTENTS

Delicious DIY

There's no better way to hold on to the taste of summer than by canning produce picked at the peak of ripeness, and when it comes to gift giving, what's better to have on hand than jars of homemade jelly or jam? Sure, you could buy these things, but making them yourself means you can use the best ingredients possible for fresh taste that's beyond compare. Also, homemade versions don't have the preservatives that store-bought varieties may contain.

When making your own foods, the right storage container is important. Follow these general guidelines:

Jams, Jellies and Preserves: For freezer jams, choose plastic containers that are meant to go in the freezer, or use glass preserving jars with no curves under the neck of the jar. Be sure to choose a size that will leave enough room for expansion. For water-bath processed jams, use glass jars specifically made for canning (regular or wide-mouth) with lids and bands.

Fruit Butter: Wide-mouth glass preserving jars or plastic containers with tight-fitting lids help fruit butter stay fresher longer.

Chutney: For chutney that will be frozen, choose plastic containers that are meant to go in the freezer, or use glass preserving jars with no curves under the neck of the jar. Be sure to choose a size that will leave enough room for expansion. For chutney that will be refrigerated only, choose wide-mouth glass preserving jars or plastic containers with tight-fitting lids.

Pickle Slices: Go for glass preserving jars (regular or wide-mouth) with lids and bands.

Pickled Vegetables: For these, it's important to use nonreactive covered containers.

Dried Vegetables: Choose tightly covered containers.

Seasoning Mixes: For these, opt for small containers with tight-fitting lids.

Dessert Mixes: Choose food-safe glass jars with screw-on lids to show off the layers.

Triple-Berry Pomegranate Freezer Jam

Fresh Herbs

Grow some fresh herbs for cooking—it's fun to be able to snip just a bit of basil to add to a salad when the container is on your windowsill. Or why not have a small pot of rosemary handy—the fragrance is amazing! Other herbs that grow well in small pots include parsley, thyme, mint and chives. Remember to snip and use the herbs often to encourage them to grow. Here are some other tips to get you started:

Purchase herbs in small pots or plant seeds in sterilized black dirt available at the garden store.

- Keep the herbs in a warm, sunny spot away from drafts.
- Water sparingly as herbs do not like wet soil.
- Feed once a month with a fertilizer labeled for use on edibles.
- Most herbs benefit from having the flowers pinched off.

Cutting Fresh Herbs

To make cutting fresh, leafy herbs easier, place several leaves on top of each other, roll tight and cut into thin strips. Then go over the layers once or twice in the opposite direction to create uniform pieces for sprinkling into your dish.

COOKING WITH HERBS

To capture the best herb flavor in all of your favorite foods, keep these tips in mind:

- Fresh herbs are milder than dried herbs, so follow the "3 to 1" rule. That simply means, when substituting fresh for dried, use three times more. When substituting dried for fresh, use one-third as much.
- In recipes with long cooking times, robust herbs (such as bay leaves, oregano, thyme, tarragon, rosemary and sage) hold up to the heat and can be added right away. But more delicate herbs (such as basil, marjoram, parsley and cilantro) should be stirred in just before serving; this is especially true when you're using fresh herbs.
- When experimenting with herbs in a four-serving recipe, start by adding 1 teaspoon of robust fresh herbs, 1 tablespoon of mild herbs or ¼ teaspoon of any dried herb. You can always add more if desired.
- Before stirring dried herbs into dishes, crush them in your hand to release their flavor and natural oils.

Shop Fresh and Local

There are loads of advantages to eating locally grown or produced food. It connects growers directly to buyers so that buyers know where their food comes from. In addition, the local economy benefits because the sales help farmers stay in business. In the United States, produce that is not local can travel nearly 1,500 miles between the farm and where you live; plus, about 40 percent of our fruit is produced overseas. Eating local means a lower environmental impact because food doesn't need to travel as far.

When it comes to freshness, produce eaten shortly after being picked can't be beat, as it has the best flavor and the most nutrients. Buying local means it's as fresh as you can get. As a bonus, food in peak season not only tastes the best, it's often the least expensive.

To find a farmers' market in your area, visit http://www.ams.usda.gov/local-food-directories/farmersmarkets

MAKING THE MOST OF THE FARMERS' MARKET

The farmers' market is a bustling scene made up of vendors, the season's best produce and visitors excited to see what's just come in and to shop. Here's a roadmap to guide you through it all, so you'll know what to expect when you arrive and can leave feeling like a seasoned pro—with all of the freshest ingredients in tow.

BRING CASH
Some vendors may be able to accept credit cards, but it's best not to count on it. Cash—small bills in particular—make for fast and easy transactions.

BRING A BAG OR TOTE
While a lot of stalls provide plastic bags, they're not the most convenient—especially if you're buying more than a handful of items. Instead, bring a bag from home to carry on your shoulder. It's more comfortable, you'll be able to fit more in it and you'll be helping the environment, too.

BROWSE THE MARKET
There's a lot to take in at the market. Before you buy, get familiar with what's available by walking around the stalls, noting prices and sampling as you go to find the best deals on the freshest items.

GO WITH A PLAN
Have a rough idea of what you're after, but stay flexible. If kale is on your list but spinach is looking better, go for that. Also, try not to overbuy, which can lead to waste.

ASK FOR SAMPLES
See something new and interesting? Don't be afraid to ask for samples; vendors are usually happy to oblige.

GO EARLY
Being there at the start means you'll get the freshest produce and the greatest selection without having to battle the morning crowd.

GET TO KNOW THE FARMERS
Most farmers and growers are excited to talk about what they do. And they're the ones with all the answers—how the food is grown, where it's grown and even ideas for how to use it.

CHECK OUT THE RULES BEFORE YOU BRING YOUR PETS
Farmers' markets can be hot and crowded spaces uncomfortable for pets, and many don't allow them because of health and safety concerns. So if you do want to bring your pet, check the market's rules first.

KNOW WHAT'S IN SEASON
Knowing what's in peak season means you'll have an idea of what will be available and at peak quality so you can plan your recipes and shopping list accordingly.

BRING A COOLER AND ICE
If you have a long drive or want to fit in a few more errands before going home, a cooler with ice will keep your carefully selected produce cool and fresh.

BEYOND THE FARMERS' MARKET

Farmers' markets are an easy and excellent way to shop for fresh, locally-grown ingredients at their seasonal best, but there are more great options for in-season favorites that you may not know about.

U-PICKS
These are farms that allow you to come during harvest time and pick your own produce. Look for ads in local newspapers or search online.

FARM STANDS
Look for farm stands along the side of the road or in parking lots of large stores. They're often selling one kind of produce brought in daily from associated farms.

FOOD CO-OPS
Food co-ops are grocery stores, usually specializing in natural and organic foods from local sources, often at great prices. They are set up as a cooperative owned and controlled by the members, although you don't typically have to be a member to shop. In some co-ops, you work a certain number of hours to be able to shop there.

COMMUNITY SUPPORTED AGRICULTURE (CSA) PROGRAMS
CSAs are another popular way to get the freshest produce directly from farmers. Consumers buy a "share" of a local farmer's produce in advance, and then receive a weekly portion of the farmer's products throughout the growing season (usually June through November). To learn more about CSAs, visit www.localharvest.org/csa.

GROCERY STORES
Many local stores feature produce from local growers when it's in season. Pay close attention to store signs, and if you don't see produce from local sources, don't be afraid to make a request.

The Fast From-Scratch Pantry

It's no secret that a well-stocked pantry is a good idea. It saves extra trips to the grocery store, inspires fresh meals and on a busy night could mean the difference between stir-fry on the fly and yet another pizza delivery.

By keeping your pantry and refrigerator stocked with the essentials, you'll easily be able to make the recipes in this cookbook and more. Use this information as a starting point and add your own favorites to the list.

SHELF-STABLE ESSENTIALS

PASTA
Sometimes dinner is as simple as combining your favorite noodles with whatever's in the fridge. Keep a wide range of pasta on hand.

RICE AND GRAINS
Whether you're adding fresh vegetables and protein to make a main dish, or stirring in herbs for a fast side, rice and grains like quinoa and farro are hard-working dinner ingredients that deserve space in your pantry.

BEANS AND LEGUMES
Dried or canned, it's worth stocking up on beans for reasons ranging from hearty pots of chili to summer salads and ethnic classics.

CANNED TOMATOES
Perfect as the base for pasta sauces, soups and stews, they're an excellent way to enjoy tomatoes year-round.

VINEGARS
Distilled (white) vinegar has many uses ranging from cooking to cleaning, while balsamic, sherry and other vinegars make excellent salad dressings.

OLIVE OIL
This staple is ideal for lightly coating vegetables before roasting, whisking with vinegar and Dijon mustard to make a vinaigrette or as a simple dip for bread.

BROTH
The backbone of soups and a smart flavor booster when boiling rice and grains, it's worth keeping the three main varieties on hand: chicken, beef and vegetable.

NUTS
Crushed to make crunchy coatings, toasted for salads or stirred into desserts, nuts have many uses.

HONEY
An equally delicious compliment to carrots, biscuits and tea, this natural sweetener works in both cooking and baking.

PEANUT BUTTER
This popular, economical and protein-packed condiment gets used in its fair share of Asian dishes as well as baked goods.

HERBS, SPICES AND GARLIC
Salt and pepper are absolutely crucial ingredients, but for more flavor interest, consider adding dried herbs like basil and thyme to your pantry, along with spices such as cumin, cinnamon and paprika.

REFRIGERATOR ESSENTIALS

EGGS
With too many uses to count, ranging from breakfast to dinner and from cooking to baking, you can't go wrong with a carton of eggs in your refrigerator at all times.

CHEESE
Whether blocks, pre-shredded, shaved or grated, cheese on hand can start or finish many dishes.

YOGURT
Plain yogurt can be spiced up as a dip to make macaroni salad and can even double as a marinade. Use it also a cup-for-cup substitute for sour cream.

CONDIMENTS
Great starters for cooking are a variety of mustards (for salad dressings), vinaigrettes and soy sauce.

BUTTER
Sometimes a pat of butter is all a bunch of steamed veggies need to shine.

CHAPTER 1

Main Meal Salads and Sandwiches

Enjoy this steakhouse favorite at home in about 20 minutes. The apple and onion add a satisfying crunch and flavor pop; glazed walnuts balance out the blue cheese beautifully.

Prep Time:
20 Minutes

Start to Finish:
20 Minutes

6 servings

Chicken Wedge Salad

6	slices bacon	1	head iceberg lettuce, cored, cut into 6 wedges
¾	cup mayonnaise	2	packages (6 oz each) refrigerated cooked chicken breast strips
⅓	cup plain yogurt		
2	tablespoons red wine vinegar	1	large apple, chopped (about 2 cups)
¾	cup crumbled blue cheese (3 oz)	¾	cup chopped red onion
		¾	cup glazed walnuts (from 3.5-oz bag)

1 In 10-inch nonstick skillet, cook bacon over medium-high heat until crisp; drain on paper towels. Crumble bacon; set aside.

2 Meanwhile, in small bowl, mix mayonnaise, yogurt, vinegar and blue cheese.

3 Place 1 lettuce wedge on each of 6 plates. Arrange chicken, apple, onion and walnuts around each wedge. Drizzle with blue cheese dressing; sprinkle with crumbled bacon.

1 Serving: Calories 540; Total Fat 42g (Saturated Fat 9g, Trans Fat 0g); Cholesterol 80mg; Sodium 600mg; Total Carbohydrate 14g (Dietary Fiber 3g); Protein 27g **Exchanges:** ½ Other Carbohydrate, 1 Vegetable, 3½ Lean Meat, 6½ Fat **Carbohydrate Choices:** 1

> TRY THIS The sweetness of the glazed nuts—which can be found near the croutons or in the baking aisle of the supermarket—adds a nice dimension to the flavors in this recipe, but you can substitute regular walnuts or pecans, if desired.

Prep Time:
25 Minutes

Start to Finish:
25 Minutes

4 servings

Orzo, rice-shaped pasta that cooks up in a flash, is a versatile pantry item to have on hand for pulling together delicious meals with whatever is in the crisper. Here, fresh herbs, mozzarella balls and chicken round out a beautiful and satisfying one-pot meal.

Orzo with Chicken and Fresh Herbs

½ cup uncooked orzo pasta (3 oz)	⅛ teaspoon pepper
1 pint (2 cups) cherry or grape tomatoes, cut in half	3 tablespoons chopped fresh basil, oregano, marjoram or thyme leaves (or a combination)
2 cloves garlic, finely chopped	2 cups cut-up cooked chicken
¼ cup olive oil	1 cup small fresh mozzarella cheese balls (about 6 oz)
3 tablespoons white wine vinegar	4 large leaves butter lettuce
½ teaspoon salt	

1 Cook and drain pasta as directed on package. Rinse with cold water to cool; drain.

2 In large bowl, mix tomatoes, garlic, oil, vinegar, salt, pepper and herbs. Add chicken, cheese and cooked pasta; toss until evenly coated.

3 To serve, spoon about 1¼ cups salad onto each lettuce leaf.

1 Serving: Calories 490; Total Fat 28g (Saturated Fat 9g, Trans Fat 0g); Cholesterol 85mg; Sodium 580mg; Total Carbohydrate 25g (Dietary Fiber 2g); Protein 35g **Exchanges:** 1½ Starch, 1 Vegetable, 4 Lean Meat, 3 Fat **Carbohydrate Choices:** 1½

You'll love this Asian-inspired chicken salad that is perfect for a family lunch or light supper.

Prep Time:
15 Minutes

Start to Finish:
15 Minutes

8 servings

Crunchy Sesame Chicken Salad

4 **cups shredded deli rotisserie chicken (from 2-lb chicken)**

1 **bag (16 oz) coleslaw mix (about 8 cups)**

2 **cups chow mein noodles**

1 **bag (8 oz) fresh sugar snap peas, strings removed (about 2 cups)**

1 **cup shredded carrots (from 10-oz bag)**

1¼ **cups Asian toasted sesame dressing (from 16-oz bottle)**

3 **medium green onions, sliced (3 tablespoons)**

1 In large serving bowl, toss all ingredients except onions until evenly coated. Sprinkle with onions.

1 Serving: Calories 370; Total Fat 21g (Saturated Fat 4g, Trans Fat 0g); Cholesterol 60mg; Sodium 810mg; Total Carbohydrate 24g (Dietary Fiber 3g); Protein 22g **Exchanges:** ½ Starch, 1 Other Carbohydrate, 3 Lean Meat, 2½ Fat **Carbohydrate Choices:** 1½

> TRY THIS For a tasty topping, try chopped wasabi- and soy sauce–flavored almonds. Look for them in the snack section of the grocery store.

This simple salad is a perfect use for a pot of basil you might be growing on your windowsill or just outside the front door. If you don't have basil to snip on the fly, however, fresh herbs from the farmers' market or grocery store will be delicious.

Prep Time:
10 Minutes

Start to Finish:
10 Minutes

4 servings

Balsamic-Mozzarella Chicken Salad

1 **container (8 oz) small fresh mozzarella cheese balls, drained**

1 **pint (2 cups) cherry tomatoes, cut in half**

2 **packages (6 oz each) refrigerated grilled chicken breast strips**

½ **cup balsamic vinaigrette dressing**

12 **leaves romaine lettuce**

Chopped fresh basil leaves, if desired

> TRY THIS
If small fresh mozzarella cheese balls (called pearls, Perline or Perlini) are unavailable, use any size fresh mozzarella and cut it into ½-inch pieces.

> INSTEAD OF
just sprinkling basil on top, add ½ cup chopped fresh basil leaves to the salad.

1 In medium bowl, gently stir cheese, tomatoes and chicken. Drizzle with dressing; toss lightly.

2 Line each of 4 plates with 3 lettuce leaves; spoon about 1¼ cups salad onto each lettuce-lined plate. Garnish with basil.

1 Serving: Calories 380; Total Fat 23g (Saturated Fat 2.5g, Trans Fat 0g); Cholesterol 95mg; Sodium 980mg; Total Carbohydrate 10g (Dietary Fiber 1g); Protein 32g **Exchanges:** ½ Other Carbohydrate, 3 Lean Meat, 1½ Medium-Fat Meat, 1½ Fat **Carbohydrate Choices:** ½

Although this salad features precooked chicken breast strips, you can use leftover cooked chicken breasts instead. Slice the breasts crosswise and mix with the peanut sauce, then continue as directed.

10 MINUTES OR LESS

Chicken Satay Salad

Prep Time:
10 Minutes

Start to Finish:
10 Minutes

4 servings

2 packages (6 oz each) refrigerated cooked chicken breast strips	1 bag (5 oz) mixed salad greens
¾ cup Thai peanut sauce	1 cup julienne carrots (from 10-oz bag)
	¼ cup chopped fresh cilantro

1 In medium microwavable bowl, mix chicken and peanut sauce. Cover; microwave on High 2 to 3 minutes or until hot.

2 Divide salad greens and carrots among 4 plates. Top evenly with chicken mixture and cilantro.

1 Serving: Calories 280; Total Fat 15g (Saturated Fat 3.5g, Trans Fat 0g); Cholesterol 55mg; Sodium 630mg; Total Carbohydrate 10g (Dietary Fiber 3g); Protein 27g **Exchanges:** ½ Starch, ½ Vegetable, 3½ Very Lean Meat, 2½ Fat **Carbohydrate Choices:** ½

Think your kids won't eat salad? They'll gobble up this delicious mix that features the satisfying crunch of shoestring potatoes.

Shoestring Potato Chicken Salad

1   **bag (12 oz) salad blend with lettuce, carrots and red cabbage**

2   **packages (6 oz each) refrigerated cooked chicken breast strips, coarsely chopped**

1   **red bell pepper, cut into ½-inch pieces**

1   **can (1¾ oz) shoestring potatoes**

¾   **cup ranch dressing**

1 In large bowl, mix salad blend, chicken, bell pepper and potatoes.

2 Divide salad among 4 plates; drizzle each with 3 tablespoons dressing.

1 Serving: Calories 370; Total Fat 26g (Saturated Fat 4.5g, Trans Fat 0g); Cholesterol 70mg; Sodium 910mg; Total Carbohydrate 11g (Dietary Fiber 3g); Protein 23g **Exchanges:** ½ Starch, 1 Vegetable, 2½ Very Lean Meat, 5 Fat **Carbohydrate Choices:** 1

> **TRY THIS** One cup chow mein noodles can be substituted for the shoestring potatoes.

A satisfying new twist on a meat-and-potatoes meal, this salad lets you combine grilled steak, potatoes and healthful greens.

Grilled Steak and Potato Salad

¾ **lb small red potatoes, cut in half**

⅔ **cup honey Dijon dressing and marinade**

1 **boneless beef sirloin steak, ¾ inch thick (¾ lb)**

¼ **teaspoon salt**

¼ **teaspoon coarse ground black pepper**

4 **cups bite-size pieces romaine lettuce**

2 **medium tomatoes, cut into thin wedges**

½ **cup thinly sliced red onion**

1 Heat gas or charcoal grill. In 2- or 2½-quart saucepan, place potatoes and enough water to cover potatoes. Heat to boiling; reduce heat to medium. Cook uncovered 5 to 8 minutes or just until potatoes are tender.

2 Drain potatoes; place in medium bowl. Add 2 tablespoons of the dressing; toss to coat. Place potatoes in grill basket (grill "wok"). Brush beef with 1 tablespoon dressing; sprinkle with salt and pepper.

3 Place beef and potatoes on grill over medium heat. Cover grill; cook 8 to 15 minutes, turning once, until potatoes are golden brown and beef is desired doneness (145°F for medium-rare). Cut beef into thin slices.

4 Divide lettuce, tomatoes and onion among 4 plates. Top with beef and potatoes; drizzle with remaining dressing. Sprinkle with additional pepper, if desired.

1 Serving: Calories 340; Total Fat 17g (Saturated Fat 3g, Trans Fat 0g); Cholesterol 50mg; Sodium 430mg; Total Carbohydrate 25g (Dietary Fiber 4g); Protein 22g **Exchanges:** ½ Starch, 1 Other Carbohydrate, 1 Vegetable, 2½ Lean Meat, 2 Fat **Carbohydrate Choices:** 1½

> TRY THIS Sprinkle each salad with 1 tablespoon crumbled blue or Gorgonzola cheese. If you like, substitute beef tenderloin for the sirloin steak.

Prep Time:
30 Minutes

Start to Finish:
30 Minutes

4 servings

Feta cheese and spinach lend Mediterranean flavors to this company-worthy salad.

Steak and Feta Spinach Salad

1   **boneless beef sirloin steak, 1½ inches thick (1 lb)**

⅔   **cup balsamic vinaigrette dressing**

1   **bag (6 oz) fresh baby spinach leaves**

1½   **cups halved cherry tomatoes**

¾   **cup crumbled tomato-basil feta cheese (3 oz)**

1   Set oven control to broil. Spray broiler pan with cooking spray. Place steak on broiler pan; brush with 1 tablespoon of the dressing. Broil with top about 4 to 6 inches from heat for 10 minutes. Turn steak over; brush with another 1 tablespoon dressing. Broil 5 to 10 minutes longer or until beef is desired doneness (145°F for medium-rare). Cover; let stand 5 minutes.

2   Meanwhile, divide spinach and tomatoes among 4 plates. Thinly slice beef across the grain; arrange over salads. Top with cheese. Drizzle with remaining dressing, about 2 tablespoons on each salad.

1 Serving: Calories 360; Total Fat 19g (Saturated Fat 4g, Trans Fat 0g); Cholesterol 80mg; Sodium 810mg; Total Carbohydrate 14g (Dietary Fiber 2g); Protein 35g **Exchanges:** ½ Starch, ½ Other Carbohydrate, 4½ Lean Meat, 1 Fat **Carbohydrate Choices:** 1

> TRY THIS Flat iron, flank steak or another tender cut can be used instead of the sirloin. Broiling times may vary if your cut of steak is thinner or thicker than 1½ inches. If you're not a spinach fan, check out other greens and salad mixes in the produce department or at your local farmers' market.

Take a trip to the topics with a ceviche salad that is short on prep time and long on flavor.

Prep Time:
20 Minutes

Start to Finish:
20 Minutes

4 servings

Chipotle Shrimp Ceviche Salad

DRESSING

- ¾ cup low-sodium vegetable juice
- 2 tablespoons fresh lime juice
- 1 chipotle chile in adobo sauce (from 7-oz can), chopped
- ½ teaspoon salt
- ¼ teaspoon coarse ground black pepper

SALAD

- 1 cup cherry tomatoes, cut in half
- 1 cup coarsely chopped hothouse (seedless) cucumber
- ¼ cup finely chopped red onion
- 2 tablespoons chopped fresh cilantro
- 4 cups torn romaine lettuce
- 1 bag (12 oz) frozen cooked deveined peeled small shrimp, thawed
- 1 medium avocado, pitted, peeled and sliced
- 16 baked tortilla chips

1 In medium bowl, mix all dressing ingredients until well blended. Stir in tomatoes, cucumber, onion and cilantro.

2 On each of 4 salad plates, place 1 cup lettuce and about 1 cup vegetable mixture. Arrange shrimp, avocado and tortilla chips on top.

1 Serving: Calories 220; Total Fat 6g (Saturated Fat 0.5g, Trans Fat 0g); Cholesterol 180mg; Sodium 1230mg; Total Carbohydrate 19g (Dietary Fiber 4g); Protein 22g **Exchanges:** 1 Starch, 1 Vegetable, 2½ Very Lean Meat, 1 Fat **Carbohydrate Choices:** 1

Enjoy this classic and versatile chef's salad with prepared Caesar dressing, or try one of the homemade dressings on pages 36–37.

Prep Time:
10 Minutes

Start to Finish:
10 Minutes

4 servings

Tuna Chef's Salad

1   **bag (10 oz) mixed salad greens (about 6 cups)**

2   **cans (5 oz each) albacore tuna in water, drained**

4   **hard-cooked eggs, sliced**

1   **cup shredded carrots (from 10-oz bag)**

¾   **cup Caesar dressing**

1   Divide salad greens among 4 plates. Top evenly with tuna, eggs and carrots. Drizzle each salad with 3 tablespoons dressing.

1 Serving: Calories 400; Total Fat 31g (Saturated Fat 6g, Trans Fat 0g); Cholesterol 245mg; Sodium 770mg; Total Carbohydrate 6g (Dietary Fiber 2g); Protein 23g **Exchanges:** 1 Vegetable, 2 Very Lean Meat, 1 Medium-Fat Meat, 5 Fat **Carbohydrate Choices:** ½

> TIME-SAVER Purchase hard-cooked eggs in the deli or dairy section of your grocery store to save time.

> TRY THIS Sliced red bell pepper can be substituted for the shredded carrots.

Sweet Potatoes

Available in varieties ranging from pale skin with light yellow flesh, to dark orange or red skin and flesh, sweet potatoes are a delicious addition to any meal. Lighter-colored sweet potatoes will have a mealy texture and not be as sweet as varieties that are darker in color. We often call these tasty gems *yams*, but true yams are a totally different vegetable and are not related to sweet potatoes.

Sweet potatoes are available year-round but are freshest and most available in the autumn months. Purchase sweet potatoes that are firm with no signs of decay. To store, keep in a cool, dark and dry place for up to two weeks.

Try one of the following ideas for these delicious vegetables.

CAJUN SWEET POTATO WEDGES On lightly greased 15x10x1-inch pan, toss peeled sweet potato wedges with 1 tablespoon olive oil, 1 teaspoon Cajun seasoning, ¼ teaspoon salt and ½ teaspoon ground cumin. Bake at 425°F for 30 to 35 minutes or until tender.

SOUR CREAM–TOPPED SWEET POTATOES Cut large x in top of baked sweet potatoes; squeeze to open slightly. Season to taste with salt and pepper. Top each potato with 2 tablespoons sour cream and 1 tablespoon chopped fresh parsley.

SWEET POTATOES WITH SUGAR SNAPS In 10-inch skillet, melt 2 tablespoons butter. Stir in 2 cups cubed, peeled sweet potatoes and cook over medium heat 2 minutes. Stir in 1 cup fresh sugar snap peas; sprinkle with ½ teaspoon garlic salt. Cook and stir 3 to 4 minutes until vegetables are fork-tender. Sprinkle with ¼ cup chopped honey-roasted peanuts.

MAPLE-GLAZED SWEET POTATOES In 10-inch skillet, melt 2 tablespoons butter. Add 2 cups sliced, peeled sweet potatoes. Cook 4 to 6 minutes or until tender. Stir in 2 tablespoons maple syrup and sprinkle with 2 tablespoons chopped fresh chives.

ASIAN SWEET POTATO AND CABBAGE SALAD In large bowl, toss 2 cups diced, cooked sweet potatoes with 2 cups shredded Napa cabbage, 1 cup julienne-cut red bell pepper, ½ cup chopped cashews and ½ cup Asian sesame dressing.

WILD RICE AND SWEET POTATOES Toss 2 cups cooked, cubed sweet potatoes with 2 cups cooked wild rice, ½ cup dried cranberries and ¼ cup sliced green onions. Add ½ cup honey mustard dressing; toss to coat. Sprinkle with ¼ cup chopped pecans or walnuts.

Trying to eat lighter as well as healthier? This calorie-smart salad is a perfect lunch or light dinner choice. Fresh chives ramp up the flavor without adding extra fat or calories.

Shrimp Salad with Zesty Dressing

⅓ cup ranch dressing

⅓ cup zesty cocktail sauce

1 bag (10 oz) torn romaine lettuce (about 6 cups)

1 cup thinly sliced hothouse (seedless) cucumber

1 cup halved cherry tomatoes

24 cooked deveined peeled large shrimp, thawed if frozen, tail shells removed

1 tablespoon chopped fresh chives

1 In small bowl, beat dressing and cocktail sauce with whisk until blended.

2 Divide lettuce, cucumber and tomatoes among 4 plates. Arrange 6 shrimp on top of each salad. Drizzle with dressing; sprinkle with chives.

1 Serving: Calories 190; Total Fat 11g (Saturated Fat 1.5g, Trans Fat 0g); Cholesterol 85mg; Sodium 510mg; Total Carbohydrate 12g (Dietary Fiber 3g); Protein 11g **Exchanges:** ½ Starch, 1 Vegetable, 1 Very Lean Meat, 2 Fat **Carbohydrate Choices:** 1

Having a small arsenal of easy, delicious dressings is within everyone's reach. You'll love making and serving this bright and herby vinaigrette.

Fresh Herb Vinaigrette Dressing

Prep Time: 10 Minutes • Start to Finish: 10 Minutes • About ³/₄ cup

½ cup olive or vegetable oil

3 tablespoons red or white wine vinegar*

1 tablespoon chopped fresh herb leaves (basil, marjoram, oregano, rosemary, tarragon or thyme)

1 tablespoon chopped fresh parsley

1 tablespoon finely chopped shallot or green onion

¾ teaspoon salt

¼ teaspoon pepper

1 In tightly covered container, shake all ingredients. Store tightly covered in refrigerator up to 1 week. Shake before serving.

*Balsamic, cider, white or plain or seasoned rice vinegar can be substituted.

1 Tablespoon: Calories 80; Total Fat 9g (Saturated Fat 1g, Trans Fat 0g); Cholesterol 0mg; Sodium 150mg; Total Carbohydrate 0g (Dietary Fiber 0g); Protein 0g
Exchanges: 2 Fat **Carbohydrate Choices:** 0

> **TRY THIS** For Blue Cheese Herb Vinaigrette Dressing, add ⅓ cup crumbled blue cheese.

> **FOR CREAMY FRESH HERB VINAIGRETTE DRESSING,** in small bowl, mix ⅓ cup mayonnaise and all ingredients with whisk until well blended.

A creamy, simple dressing perfect for leafy greens, dipping vegetables or as a potato topper.

A flavorful topping perfect for sautéed vegetables and Asian-inspired salads.

Buttermilk Ranch Dressing

Prep Time: 10 Minutes • Start to Finish:
10 Minutes • 1¾ cups

- ¾ cup mayonnaise or salad dressing
- 1 clove garlic, finely chopped
- ½ cup buttermilk
- 1 teaspoon parsley flakes
- ½ teaspoon dried minced onion
- ½ teaspoon salt
- Dash freshly ground pepper

1 In small bowl, mix all ingredients. Store tightly covered in refrigerator up to 5 days. Stir before serving.

1 Tablespoon: Calories 60; Total Fat 7g (Saturated Fat 1g, Trans Fat 0g); Cholesterol 0mg; Sodium 110mg; Total Carbohydrate 0g (Dietary Fiber 0g); Protein 0g
Exchanges: 1½ Fat **Carbohydrate Choices:** 0

> **TRY THIS** For Buttermilk Ranch-Parmesan Dressing, add ⅓ cup grated Parmesan cheese and ½ teaspoon paprika.

> **IF YOU HAVE TIME,** refrigerate the dressing for 2 hours before serving for the flavors to blend.

Asian Dressing

Prep Time: 10 Minutes • Start to Finish:
10 Minutes • 1 cup

- ⅓ cup rice vinegar, white vinegar or cider vinegar
- ¼ cup vegetable oil
- 3 tablespoons soy sauce
- 2 tablespoons dry sherry or apple juice
- 1 teaspoon dark sesame oil
- 1 teaspoon grated gingerroot or ¼ teaspoon ground ginger
- 1 tablespoon sesame seed, toasted*
- 1 teaspoon sugar

1 In tightly covered container, shake all ingredients. Store tightly covered in refrigerator up to 1 week. Shake before serving.

*To toast sesame seed, sprinkle in ungreased skillet. Cook over medium-low heat 5 to 7 minutes, stirring frequently until browning begins, then stirring constantly until golden brown. Toast a whole 2-ounce package or jar (about ½ cup) and store in the freezer. You can also buy jars of toasted sesame seed; store it the same way.

1 Tablespoon: Calories 35; Total Fat 3.5g (Saturated Fat 0g, Trans Fat 0g); Cholesterol 0mg; Sodium 170mg; Total Carbohydrate 0g (Dietary Fiber 0g); Protein 0g
Exchanges: ½ Fat **Carbohydrate Choices:** 0

> **TRY THIS** If you like a sweeter dressing, add another teaspoon of sugar.

These flavorful grilled sandwiches combine prepared pesto and fresh basil for a one-two basil punch that serves as a perfect complement for the chicken sausages.

Prep Time:
30 Minutes

Start to Finish:
30 Minutes

4 sandwiches

Toasted Pesto–Chicken Sausage Sandwiches

1   **package (12 oz) fully cooked smoked chicken and apple sausages**

3   **tablespoons olive oil**

½   **cup refrigerated basil pesto (from 7-oz container)**

2   **tablespoons mayonnaise or salad dressing**

8   **slices (½ inch thick) Italian bread**

4   **slices (¾ oz each) provolone cheese**

1   **large tomato, cut into 8 thin slices**

16   **fresh basil leaves**

1   Cut sausages almost in half crosswise, then in half lengthwise. In 12-inch skillet, heat 1 tablespoon of the oil over medium-high heat. Cook sausages in oil 5 to 7 minutes, turning occasionally, until golden brown. Remove from skillet; set aside.

2   In small bowl, mix pesto and mayonnaise. Brush one side of bread slices with remaining 2 tablespoons oil. Spread pesto mayonnaise on plain side of 4 of the bread slices.

3   On each slice spread with pesto mayonnaise, place 1 cheese slice, 2 tomato slices, 4 basil leaves and 1 cooked sausage. Top with remaining bread slices, oiled side up. Heat same skillet or a griddle over medium-high heat. Add sandwiches; cook 3 to 5 minutes, turning once, until golden brown and cheese is melted.

1 Sandwich: Calories 620; Total Fat 45g (Saturated Fat 11g, Trans Fat 0.5g); Cholesterol 80mg; Sodium 1340mg; Total Carbohydrate 28g (Dietary Fiber 2g); Protein 26g **Exchanges:** 1½ Starch, ½ Vegetable, 3 High-Fat Meat, 4 Fat **Carbohydrate Choices:** 2

> FRESH FACT Cutting the sausages almost in half crosswise serves two purposes. First, they don't curl up when cooked, so they will lay flat in the sandwiches. Second, because the sausages are basically still in one long piece, they won't fall out of the bread when turning the sandwiches in the skillet.

Prep Time:
30 Minutes

Start to Finish:
30 Minutes

4 burgers

Your family will love these Greek-flavored chicken burgers with the zip of fresh, homemade Tzatziki sauce. If you want, prepare extra for a refreshing vegetable dip.

Greek Chicken Burgers with Tzatziki Sauce

TZATZIKI SAUCE

- 1 medium cucumber
- ½ cup fat-free plain Greek yogurt
- 2 tablespoons chopped onion
- 2 teaspoons chopped fresh mint leaves

BURGERS

- 1 lb ground chicken breast
- 1 cup chopped fresh spinach leaves
- ¼ cup chopped pitted kalamata olives
- 1 tablespoon cornstarch
- 1 tablespoon chopped fresh oregano leaves
- 2 cloves garlic, finely chopped
- ¼ teaspoon salt
- ¼ teaspoon pepper
- 2 whole-wheat pita (pocket) breads (6 inch), cut in half to form pockets
- ½ cup chopped tomato (1 small)

1 Set oven control to broil. Cut 12 slices from cucumber; set aside. Chop enough remaining cucumber to equal ½ cup; place in small bowl. Stir in yogurt, onion and mint. Refrigerate until serving time.

2 In large bowl, mix chicken, spinach, olives, cornstarch, oregano, garlic, salt and pepper. Shape mixture into 4 oval patties, ½ inch thick.

3 Place patties on broiler pan. Broil with tops about 5 inches from heat 10 to 12 minutes, turning once, until thermometer inserted in center of patties reads 165°F.

4 Place 1 burger in each pita half. Add tomato and 3 reserved cucumber slices to each pita half. Serve with tzatziki sauce.

1 Burger: Calories 270; Total Fat 6g (Saturated Fat 1.5g, Trans Fat 0g); Cholesterol 70mg; Sodium 460mg; Total Carbohydrate 24g (Dietary Fiber 3g); Protein 32g **Exchanges:** 1½ Starch, 1 Vegetable, 2½ Very Lean Meat, 1 Lean Meat **Carbohydrate Choices:** 1½

> **TRY THIS** Sprinkle 1 tablespoon crumbled feta cheese in each pita half.

You can whip up these delicious chicken sandwiches faster than you can pick up an order in the drive-through, and the raisin-nut bread adds a unique, sweet and nutty flavor.

Prep Time:
10 Minutes

Start to Finish:
10 Minutes

4 sandwiches

Fast and Fresh Chicken Sandwiches

8   slices rustic raisin-nut or cranberry-nut bread

½   cup mascarpone cheese

4   medium green onions, chopped (¼ cup)

4   teaspoons chopped fresh dill weed

1   package (9 oz) thin-sliced cooked chicken breast

1 On one side of each bread slice, spread 1 tablespoon cheese. On 4 slices, evenly sprinkle onions. On remaining 4 slices, evenly sprinkle dill. Divide chicken among onion-topped bread slices; cover with dill-topped bread slices.

1 Sandwich: Calories 260; Total Fat 4.5g (Saturated Fat 1g, Trans Fat 0.5g); Cholesterol 35mg; Sodium 1000mg; Total Carbohydrate 34g (Dietary Fiber 3g); Protein 20g **Exchanges:** 1½ Starch, 1 Other Carbohydrate, 2 Very Lean Meat, ½ Fat **Carbohydrate Choices:** 2

Food doesn't get more comforting than this chicken-filled take on classic grilled cheese. Be sure to serve these with a glass of cold milk to enjoy a nostalgic twist on dinner.

Cheddar-Chicken Grilled Cheese Sandwiches

Prep Time:
10 Minutes
Start to Finish:
10 Minutes
2 sandwiches

4 slices sourdough or other rustic whole-grain bread

2 tablespoons apple butter

4 slices (¾ to 1 oz each) sharp Cheddar cheese

4 oz thinly sliced cooked chicken breast

2 tablespoons butter, softened

1 On one side of 2 bread slices, evenly spread apple butter. Top each with 1 slice of cheese, half of the chicken, a second slice of cheese and remaining bread slices.

2 In 10-inch nonstick skillet, melt 1 tablespoon of the butter over medium-low heat. Place sandwiches in skillet. Spread tops of bread with remaining 1 tablespoon butter. Cook 5 minutes, turning once, until cheese is melted and bread is golden brown.

1 Sandwich: Calories 740; Total Fat 30g (Saturated Fat 17g, Trans Fat 1g); Cholesterol 100mg; Sodium 1850mg; Total Carbohydrate 83g (Dietary Fiber 3g); Protein 35g **Exchanges:** 4½ Starch, 1 Other Carbohydrate, 3 Lean Meat, 3½ Fat **Carbohydrate Choices:** 5½

> **TRY THIS** Easily change up this sandwich by using different kinds of cheese, such as Monterey Jack or Muenster.

These elegant crostini make a super-fast meal or welcome appetizer for last-minute guests. They also provide an unexpected way to use up leftover chicken.

Prep Time:
10 Minutes

Start to Finish:
10 Minutes

4 servings
(2 crostini each)

Chicken-Fig Crostini

¾ **cup fig spread or preserves**
⅓ **cup finely chopped shallots**
3 **tablespoons balsamic vinegar**
2 **tablespoons olive oil**

2 **cups mixed baby salad greens**
2 **cups shredded cooked chicken**
8 **slices rustic Italian bread, toasted**
½ **cup crumbled chèvre (goat) cheese**
    (2 oz)

1 In small bowl, mix fig spread, shallots, vinegar and oil. In medium bowl, toss salad greens and chicken with ½ cup of the fig dressing.

2 Divide greens and chicken mixture among toasted bread slices; drizzle with remaining fig dressing. Top with goat cheese.

1 Serving: Calories 580; Total Fat 18g (Saturated Fat 6g, Trans Fat 0.5g); Cholesterol 70mg; Sodium 490mg; Total Carbohydrate 75g (Dietary Fiber 3g); Protein 28g **Exchanges:** 2½ Starch, 2 Other Carbohydrate, 1 Vegetable, 2½ Lean Meat, 2 Fat **Carbohydrate Choices:** 5

The secret to getting sandwich-shop crusty paninis is to be sure to let the panini press preheat for a solid five minutes. Many models have "ready" lights that will come on, or change color, when the press is hot enough to get a great sear on the sandwiches.

Prep Time:
20 Minutes

Start to Finish:
20 Minutes

4 servings
(½ panini each)

Smoky Chicken Melt Paninis

4 **large slices sourdough bread (½ inch thick)**	¼ **cup cooked real bacon bits (from 3-oz jar)**
2 **tablespoons butter, softened**	6 **thin slices tomato**
4 **oz smoky Cheddar cheese, sliced**	2 **thin slices onion, separated into rings**
1½ **cups shredded cooked chicken**	

1 Heat panini maker or closed contact grill for 5 minutes. Meanwhile, spread one side of each bread slice with butter. On unbuttered side of 2 slices, arrange half of the cheese. Top evenly with chicken, bacon, tomato, onion and remaining cheese. Top with remaining 2 bread slices, buttered sides up.

2 Place sandwiches in panini maker. Close cover, pressing down lightly; cook 3 to 5 minutes or until bread is toasted and cheese is melted. Cut each sandwich in half to serve.

1 Serving: Calories 570; Total Fat 22g (Saturated Fat 12g, Trans Fat 1g); Cholesterol 100mg; Sodium 1110mg; Total Carbohydrate 56g (Dietary Fiber 2g); Protein 36g **Exchanges:** 3 Starch, ½ Other Carbohydrate, 1½ Very Lean Meat, 1½ Lean Meat, 1 Medium-Fat Meat, 2 Fat **Carbohydrate Choices:** 4

Mild white fish is a versatile have-on-hand ingredient similar to boneless, skinless chicken breasts. Keep a bag in the freezer and you'll always be ready for easy meals like these flavorful fish rolls.

Prep Time:
25 Minutes

Start to Finish:
25 Minutes

4 sandwiches

Angry Tilapia Rolls

1 tablespoon Creole seasoning

2 teaspoons garlic-pepper blend

4 tilapia fillets or other mild-flavored, medium-firm fish fillets (3 to 4 oz each)

1 loaf (12 oz) baguette French bread (about 22 inches long)

1 cup chopped hearts of romaine lettuce

4 slices (½ oz each) Colby cheese

¼ cup ranch dressing

1 to 2 teaspoons red pepper sauce

1 Heat oven to 375°F. Line cookie sheet with foil. In 1-gallon resealable food-storage plastic bag, mix Creole seasoning and garlic-pepper blend. Cut each fish fillet lengthwise into 3 or 4 strips, about 1 to 1½ inches wide; place in bag. Seal bag; shake to coat.

2 Place fish on cookie sheet. Bake 12 to 15 minutes or until fish flakes easily with fork. Let stand 5 minutes.

3 Meanwhile, cut French bread crosswise into 4 pieces; cut each piece lengthwise in half to within ½ inch of bottom. Fill each with ¼ cup lettuce, 1 cheese slice and 2 to 3 pieces of fish; drizzle fish with 1 tablespoon dressing and ¼ to ½ teaspoon red pepper sauce.

1 Sandwich: Calories 450; Total Fat 15g (Saturated Fat 4.5g, Trans Fat 0g); Cholesterol 65mg; Sodium 1520mg; Total Carbohydrate 50g (Dietary Fiber 2g); Protein 29g **Exchanges:** 2½ Starch, 1 Other Carbohydrate, 2½ Very Lean Meat, ½ High-Fat Meat, 1½ Fat **Carbohydrate Choices:** 3

> **TIME-SAVER** Have frozen tilapia fillets on hand? Be sure to thaw them in the refrigerator the night before you plan to make this recipe and pat them dry before using.

These delicious beef burritos taste so much better than frozen burritos and come together quickly from leftovers and pantry items. They're perfect for an on-the-go meal.

Prep Time:
15 Minutes

Start to Finish:
15 Minutes

8 burritos

Beef Burritos

2	cups shredded cooked beef	2	cups shredded lettuce
1	cup refried beans (from 16-oz can)	2	medium tomatoes, chopped (1½ cups)
8	flour tortillas (9 or 10 inch)	1	cup shredded Cheddar cheese (4 oz)

1 In 2 (1-quart) saucepans, heat beef and beans separately over medium heat 2 to 5 minutes, stirring occasionally, until hot. Meanwhile, heat tortillas as directed on package.

2 Spoon about ¼ cup beef on center of each tortilla. Spoon about 2 tablespoons beans onto beef. Top each with ¼ cup lettuce, 3 tablespoons tomatoes and 2 tablespoons cheese.

3 Fold one end of tortilla up about 1 inch over filling; fold right and left sides over folded end, overlapping. Fold remaining end down.

1 Burrito: Calories 390; Total Fat 15g (Saturated Fat 6g, Trans Fat 1g); Cholesterol 45mg; Sodium 530mg; Total Carbohydrate 44g (Dietary Fiber 4g); Protein 20g **Exchanges:** 3 Starch, 1½ Medium-Fat Meat, 1 Fat **Carbohydrate Choices:** 3

> TRY THIS Shredded, cooked chicken can be substituted for the beef and Monterey Jack cheese for the Cheddar.

Round out this meal with a mixed greens or fresh fruit salad. To save time, pick up cut-up fruit from the deli.

Prep Time:
10 Minutes

Start to Finish:
10 Minutes

4 sandwiches

Garlic-Beef Sandwiches

½ cup garlic-herb mayonnaise (from 12-oz bottle)

4 demi French baguette rolls (5 to 6 inch), cut in half horizontally

1 lb thinly sliced cooked roast beef (from deli)

1 cup fresh spinach leaves

3 plum (Roma) tomatoes, thinly sliced

1 Spread mayonnaise over cut surfaces of each roll. On roll bottoms, layer beef, spinach and tomatoes. Cover with roll tops. Secure with toothpicks; cut each sandwich in half to serve.

1 Sandwich: Calories 460; Total Fat 12g (Saturated Fat 2.5g, Trans Fat 0g); Cholesterol 65mg; Sodium 1920mg; Total Carbohydrate 56g (Dietary Fiber 2g); Protein 33g **Exchanges:** 2½ Starch, 1 Other Carbohydrate, ½ Vegetable, 3½ Lean Meat **Carbohydrate Choices:** 4

> TRY THIS If you can't find the demi baguettes, use a regular size baguette French bread and cut it into 4 serving portions.

Toasting the buns means that they will absorb the delicious sauces from the meat, but won't get soggy.

Prep Time:
30 Minutes

Start to Finish:
30 Minutes

4 servings
(1 sandwich and
3 tablespoons
sauce each)

Teriyaki-Pineapple Pork Sandwiches

1 **tablespoon vegetable oil**	1 **teaspoon garlic-pepper blend**
1 **medium red bell pepper, cut into 2-inch strips**	½ **cup teriyaki sauce (from 10-oz bottle)**
1 **lb boneless pork loin chops, cut into thin strips**	1 **can (8 oz) pineapple slices in juice, drained, ⅓ cup juice reserved**
1 **medium onion, cut lengthwise in half, then cut into thin wedges**	4 **onion buns, split**

1 In 12-inch nonstick skillet, heat oil over medium-high heat. Cook bell pepper in oil 3 to 4 minutes, stirring frequently, until crisp-tender. Remove from skillet; set aside.

2 In same skillet, cook pork, onion and garlic-pepper blend over medium-high heat 7 to 9 minutes, stirring occasionally, until pork is no longer pink in center. Stir in teriyaki sauce and reserved pineapple juice; cook about 2 minutes, stirring occasionally, until hot.

3 Meanwhile, set oven control to broil. On cookie sheet, place buns cut sides up. Broil with tops 5 to 6 inches from heat 1 to 2 minutes or until lightly toasted.

4 Using slotted spoon, fill buns with pork mixture. Top with pineapple slices and bell pepper. Spoon teriyaki-pineapple sauce from skillet into small bowls; serve with sandwiches for dipping.

1 Serving: Calories 390; Total Fat 14g (Saturated Fat 4g, Trans Fat 0g); Cholesterol 70mg; Sodium 1700mg; Total Carbohydrate 37g (Dietary Fiber 2g); Protein 30g **Exchanges:** 1 Starch, ½ Fruit, ½ Other Carbohydrate, 1 Vegetable, 2½ Lean Meat, 1 Medium-Fat Meat **Carbohydrate Choices:** 2½

> GO-WITH IDEA For a super-fast supper, pick up coleslaw and cut-up fresh fruit from the grocery store salad bar to serve with these sandwiches.

Who says French toast has to be sweet? This savory foil on everyone's favorite brunch treat makes a fun and welcome dinner. French toast—sweet or savory—is a perfect way to keep from wasting day-old bread.

Prep Time:
20 Minutes

Start to Finish:
20 Minutes

6 sandwiches

Ham and Cheese French Toast Sandwiches

1 cup milk	2 tablespoons Dijon mustard
⅓ cup Original Bisquick™ mix	6 oz thinly sliced cooked ham (from deli)
2 teaspoons vanilla	1½ cups shredded mild Cheddar cheese (6 oz)
4 eggs	2 tablespoons butter
12 slices (½-inch thick) day-old ciabatta or French bread	Powdered sugar, if desired

1 In shallow dish, stir milk, Bisquick mix, vanilla and eggs with fork or whisk until blended. Spread inside of each of 6 slices of bread with 1 teaspoon mustard. Top with ham, cheese and remaining bread slices.

2 Heat griddle or skillet over medium heat; melt butter on griddle. Dip sandwiches in egg mixture, coating both sides. Place sandwiches on hot griddle; cook about 5 minutes, turning once, until golden brown.

3 Cut sandwiches in half diagonally to serve; sprinkle with powdered sugar.

1 Sandwich: Calories 400; Total Fat 21g (Saturated Fat 11g, Trans Fat 0.5g); Cholesterol 180mg; Sodium 1000mg; Total Carbohydrate 29g (Dietary Fiber 1g); Protein 23g **Exchanges:** 1 Starch, 1 Other Carbohydrate, 1 Very Lean Meat, ½ Lean Meat, ½ Medium-Fat Meat, 1 High-Fat Meat, 1½ Fat **Carbohydrate Choices:** 2

> TRY THIS For a sweet and savory taste, serve the French toast sandwiches with your favorite jam or preserves.

Prep Time:
20 Minutes

Start to Finish:
20 Minutes

2 sandwiches

A great spin on the more expected breakfast sandwich with an English muffin, these grilled bagel sandwiches are delicious for breakfast, but perfect for any meal. For breakfast on a busy morning, make the paninis and then wrap them, still hot, in aluminum foil.

Breakfast Panini

2	eggs	2	thin slices onion
½	teaspoon salt-free seasoning blend	4	thin slices reduced-sodium cooked ham (from deli)
2	tablespoons chopped fresh chives		
2	whole-wheat thin bagels	2	thin slices reduced-fat Cheddar cheese
2	slices tomato		

1 Spray 8-inch skillet with cooking spray; heat over medium heat. In medium bowl, beat eggs, seasoning blend and chives with whisk until well mixed. Pour into skillet. As eggs begin to set at bottom and side, gently lift cooked portions with spatula so that thin, uncooked portion can flow to bottom. Avoid constant stirring. Cook 3 to 4 minutes or until eggs are thickened throughout but still moist. Remove from heat.

2 Heat panini maker or closed contact grill for 5 minutes. Meanwhile, spoon scrambled eggs onto bagel bottoms. Top each with 1 tomato slice, 1 onion slice, 2 ham slices and 1 cheese slice. Cover with bagel tops.

3 Place sandwiches in panini maker. Close cover, pressing down lightly; cook 2 to 3 minutes or until bagels are toasted and cheese is melted.

1 Sandwich: Calories 300; Total Fat 11g (Saturated Fat 4.5g, Trans Fat 0g); Cholesterol 205mg; Sodium 490mg; Total Carbohydrate 32g (Dietary Fiber 3g); Protein 18g **Exchanges:** 1½ Starch, ½ Other Carbohydrate, 1 Very Lean Meat, 1 Lean Meat, 1½ Fat **Carbohydrate Choices:** 2

> TRY THIS Spread cut sides of each bagel with 1½ teaspoons mayonnaise and 1 teaspoon Dijon mustard.

Prep Time:
25 Minutes

Start to Finish:
25 Minutes

2 sandwiches

Some fresh, cold fruit is a beautiful accompaniment to these hearty grilled sandwiches. Try mixed berries for a fun treat.

Scrambled Egg–Grilled Cheese Sandwiches

4 **eggs**	2 **oz Havarti or dill Havarti cheese, cut into 4 slices**
1 **tablespoon milk**	4 **slices tomato**
½ **teaspoon salt**	1 **tablespoon butter, softened**
½ **teaspoon pepper**	
4 **slices sourdough bread (about ½ inch thick)**	

1   In medium bowl, beat eggs, milk, salt and pepper with fork or whisk until well mixed. Heat 10-inch nonstick skillet over medium heat. Pour egg mixture into skillet. As mixture begins to set at bottom and side, gently lift cooked portions with spatula so that thin, uncooked portion can flow to bottom. Avoid constant stirring. Cook 3 to 4 minutes or until eggs are thickened throughout but still moist.

2   Spoon scrambled eggs onto 2 of the bread slices. Top with cheese, tomato and remaining bread slices. Spread ¾ teaspoon butter over each top slice of bread.

3   Wipe out skillet; heat over medium-high heat. Add sandwiches, buttered sides down, to skillet. Spread remaining butter over top slices of bread. Cook 4 to 5 minutes or until bottoms are golden brown. Turn; cook 4 to 5 minutes longer or until bottoms are golden brown and cheese is melted. Cut sandwiches in half to serve.

1 Sandwich Calories 550; Total Fat 28g (Saturated Fat 14g, Trans Fat 0.5g); Cholesterol 420mg; Sodium 1360mg; Total Carbohydrate 45g (Dietary Fiber 2g); Protein 28g **Exchanges:** 2 Starch, 1 Other Carbohydrate, 2 Medium-Fat Meat, 1 High-Fat Meat, 2 Fat **Carbohydrate Choices:** 3

You won't miss the meat in these scrumptious burgers! You'll love the smoky taste of the spices and the pile-'em-high toppings. If you like, serve the burgers and toppings in buns or pita bread.

Prep Time:
30 Minutes

Start to Finish:
30 Minutes

4 burgers

Monster Veggie Burgers

1   **can (15 oz) chickpeas or garbanzo beans, drained, rinsed**

1   **egg**

1   **clove garlic, finely chopped**

1   **teaspoon smoked paprika**

½   **teaspoon ground coriander**

½   **teaspoon ground cumin**

½   **teaspoon coarse (kosher or sea) salt**

1   **cup chopped fresh spinach leaves**

½   **cup shredded carrots (from 10-oz bag)**

2   **tablespoons chopped fresh cilantro**

¾   **cup panko crispy bread crumbs**

2   **tablespoons vegetable oil**

Toppings (avocado halves, cilantro leaves, cucumber slices, tomato slices, bell pepper strips, lettuce leaves), if desired

Sauces (spicy mustard, Sriracha, ketchup, citrus vinaigrette), if desired

Any buns about 4 inches in diameter, split horizontally (if desired)

> TRY THIS The patties can be cooked on the grill instead of in a skillet. Heat gas or charcoal grill. Spray sheet of heavy-duty foil with cooking spray; place patties on foil. Place on grill over medium-high heat. Cover grill; cook 8 to 10 minutes, turning once, until brown and crisp.

1   In food processor, place chickpeas, egg, garlic, paprika, coriander, cumin and salt. Cover; process with on-and-off pulses about 45 seconds or until nearly smooth.

2   In medium bowl, stir together bean mixture, spinach, carrots and chopped cilantro until well combined. Stir in bread crumbs. Shape mixture into 4 patties, about 3½ inches in diameter and ½ inch thick.

3   In 10-inch nonstick skillet, heat oil over medium heat. Cook patties in oil 8 to 10 minutes, turning once, until brown and crisp.

4   Serve veggie burgers stacked with toppings and drizzled with sauce.

1 Burger (Without Toppings): Calories 350; Total Fat 13g (Saturated Fat 1g, Trans Fat 0g); Cholesterol 55mg; Sodium 370mg; Total Carbohydrate 46g (Dietary Fiber 7g); Protein 13g **Exchanges:** 2½ Starch, 1½ Vegetable, ½ Very Lean Meat, 2 Fat **Carbohydrate Choices:** 3

> GO-WITH IDEA Add even more veggies to these burgers by serving with a fresh vegetable salsa. In medium bowl, mix 1 cup coarsely chopped red or yellow bell pepper, ½ cup thinly sliced cucumber, ¼ cup slivered white onion and ¼ cup cilantro leaves. Stir in 1 tablespoon fresh lime juice, 1 tablespoon olive oil and salt and pepper to taste. Makes about 2 cups.

These burgers are great on their own, but go ahead and add some seasonal fresh fruit on the side.

Prep Time:
25 Minutes

Start to Finish:
25 Minutes

4 burgers

Veggie and Bean Burgers

½	cup small fresh broccoli florets	1	clove garlic, peeled
2	oz fresh mushrooms (about 4 medium)	½	teaspoon seasoned salt
½	small red bell pepper, cut into large pieces	1	teaspoon dried chopped onion
½	cup cooked white or brown rice	⅓	cup seasoned dry bread crumbs
1	can (15 oz) chickpeas or garbanzo beans, drained, rinsed	3	tablespoons vegetable oil
1	egg	4	whole-wheat burger buns, split
			Toppings (Cheddar cheese slices, lettuce, tomato slices, onion slices, mayonnaise), if desired

1 In food processor, place broccoli, mushrooms and bell pepper. Cover; process, using quick on-and-off pulses, to finely chop vegetables (do not puree). Remove vegetables to medium bowl; stir in rice.

2 Add chickpeas, egg, garlic and seasoned salt to food processor. Cover; process until smooth. Stir chickpea mixture, dried chopped onion and bread crumbs into vegetable mixture. Shape mixture into 4 patties, about ½ inch thick.

3 In 10-inch nonstick skillet, heat oil over medium-high heat. Cook patties in oil 8 to 10 minutes, turning once, until brown and crisp. Serve in buns with toppings.

1 Burger: Calories 460; Total Fat 16g (Saturated Fat 2.5g, Trans Fat 0g); Cholesterol 55mg; Sodium 540mg; Total Carbohydrate 61g (Dietary Fiber 9g); Protein 17g **Exchanges:** 3½ Starch, 2 Vegetable, 2 Fat **Carbohydrate Choices:** 4

> **TIME-SAVER** Cook instant rice using the stovetop method, which is ready in about 5 minutes. Or, this recipe is a great way to use up leftover cooked long-grain rice or any type of rice you have on hand.

> **TRY THIS** For Veggie and Bean "Meatballs," heat oven to 400°F. Generously spray 15x10x1-inch pan with cooking spray. Shape vegetable mixture into 16 balls; place in pan. Generously spray tops of balls with cooking spray. Bake about 20 minutes or until crisp. Serve with cheese sauce or tomato pasta sauce (any meatless variety).

This recipe makes a great weeknight meal for two. If you're feeding more, just double or triple the recipe.

Prep Time:
20 Minutes

Start to Finish:
20 Minutes

2 sandwiches

Portabella Muffuletta Sandwiches

OLIVE SALAD

¼ cup chopped celery

3 tablespoons chopped pimiento-stuffed green olives

1 tablespoon reduced-fat mayonnaise or salad dressing

SANDWICHES

6 oz fresh portabella mushrooms, cut into ½-inch-thick slices

1 to 2 teaspoons olive or vegetable oil

⅛ teaspoon garlic powder

2 French rolls (6 inch), split

2 slices (¾ oz each) provolone or mozzarella cheese

½ medium tomato, thinly sliced

1 In small bowl, mix olive salad ingredients; set aside.

2 Spray broiler pan with cooking spray. Place mushroom slices on pan. In small bowl, mix oil and garlic powder. Brush half of the oil mixture on mushrooms. Broil 4 to 6 inches from heat 5 to 6 minutes or until mushrooms are tender, turning and brushing with remaining oil mixture halfway through cooking. Remove mushrooms from pan.

3 Place rolls, cut sides up, on broiler pan. Broil 4 to 6 inches from heat 30 to 60 seconds or until golden brown. Place cheese on roll bottoms. Top with mushrooms, olive salad and tomato slices. Cover with roll tops.

1 Sandwich: Calories 330; Total Fat 16g (Saturated Fat 5g, Trans Fat 0g); Cholesterol 15mg; Sodium 780mg; Total Carbohydrate 33g (Dietary Fiber 3g); Protein 13g **Exchanges:** 1 Starch, ½ Other Carbohydrate, 2 Vegetable, 1 Medium-Fat Meat, 2 Fat **Carbohydrate Choices:** 2

This sandwich is a great starting point. Feel free to get creative with the greens and cheese to make your own combinations based on what your family loves and what pantry items you have on hand.

Prep Time:
15 Minutes

Start to Finish:
15 Minutes

4 sandwiches

Fontina Panini with Spinach

8 slices (½ inch thick) crusty Italian bread	**1** cup loosely packed fresh spinach leaves
2 tablespoons honey mustard	**½** cup drained roasted red bell peppers (from a jar), cut into strips
2 medium green onions, sliced (2 tablespoons)	**4** oz fontina cheese, cut into ⅛-inch-thick slices

1 Heat panini maker or closed contact grill for 5 minutes. Spread one side of each bread slice with mustard. Sprinkle onions over 4 slices of bread; layer with spinach, roasted peppers and cheese. Top with remaining bread slices.

2 Place sandwiches in panini maker. Close cover, pressing down lightly; cook 2 to 3 minutes or until bread is toasted and cheese is melted. Cut each sandwich in half to serve.

1 Sandwich: Calories 260; Total Fat 13g (Saturated Fat 6g, Trans Fat 0.5g); Cholesterol 35mg; Sodium 570mg; Total Carbohydrate 25g (Dietary Fiber 2g); Protein 11g **Exchanges:** 1½ Starch, 1 Medium-Fat Meat, 1½ Fat **Carbohydrate Choices:** 1½

> TRY THIS For great flavor and crunch, add a few chopped pecans with the green onions.

> IF FONTINA is not available, substitute Gouda cheese.

CHAPTER 2

Savory Soups and Stews

Canned beans, precooked chicken and Israeli couscous create a fast, exotic soup with international flavors. Make a double batch for an easy get-together with friends.

Prep Time:
30 Minutes

Start to Finish:
30 Minutes

6 servings
(1¼ cups each)

Moroccan Chicken Soup

1 tablespoon olive oil	¼ teaspoon ground cinnamon
2 cups sliced carrots (about 4 medium)	¼ teaspoon pepper
1 large red bell pepper, cut into ¾-inch pieces	1 can (15 oz) chickpeas (garbanzo beans), drained, rinsed
2 cloves garlic, finely chopped	⅓ cup uncooked Israeli couscous
5 cups chicken broth	2 cups shredded deli rotisserie chicken (from 2-lb chicken)
1½ teaspoons ground cumin	Fresh cilantro leaves, if desired

1 In 4-quart saucepan or Dutch oven, heat oil over medium heat. Cook carrots, bell pepper and garlic in oil about 3 minutes, stirring frequently, until carrots are crisp-tender.

2 Stir in remaining ingredients except chicken and cilantro. Heat to boiling; reduce heat. Simmer uncovered 5 minutes, stirring occasionally. Stir in chicken; simmer 5 minutes longer or until carrots are tender. Sprinkle individual servings with cilantro.

1 Serving: Calories 260; Total Fat 8g (Saturated Fat 1.5g, Trans Fat 0g); Cholesterol 40mg; Sodium 1130mg; Total Carbohydrate 27g (Dietary Fiber 5g); Protein 19g **Exchanges:** 1 Starch, ½ Other Carbohydrate, 1 Vegetable, 2 Very Lean Meat, 1½ Fat **Carbohydrate Choices:** 2

> FRESH FACT Israeli couscous, also called pearl couscous, is made from semolina or wheat flour. Larger than traditional couscous, it is cooked more like pasta and has a chewy texture, similar to barley.

> GO-WITH IDEA For a bold taste experience, top each serving with a spoonful of harissa, the spicy and complex Middle Eastern condiment. Offer warm naan on the side.

Fresh broccoli ups the vegetable quotient in this traditional comfort soup. For extra warmth and hominess, the broth is thickened slightly to create a heartier meal.

Prep Time:
25 Minutes

Start to Finish:
25 Minutes

6 servings
(1⅓ cups each)

Chunky Vegetable–Chicken Noodle Bowl

1	**bag (12 oz) frozen home-style egg noodles**
3½	**cups chicken broth (from 32-oz carton)**
4	**medium carrots, cut diagonally into ½-inch pieces (1½ cups)**

1	**medium onion, cut lengthwise in half, then cut into thin wedges**
1	**teaspoon garlic-pepper blend**
1½	**cups small fresh broccoli florets**
1	**tablespoon cornstarch**
2	**cups cut-up cooked chicken**

1 Cook and drain noodles as directed on package. Meanwhile, in 3-quart saucepan, heat 2½ cups of the broth to boiling. Stir in carrots, onion and garlic-pepper blend; reduce heat to medium. Cover; cook 6 minutes. Stir in broccoli; cook 2 to 4 minutes longer or until vegetables are crisp-tender.

2 In small bowl, mix remaining 1 cup broth and the cornstarch; stir into vegetable mixture. Cook and stir over medium heat until thickened. Increase heat to high. Stir in cooked noodles and chicken. Cook and stir until thoroughly heated.

1 Serving: Calories 270; Total Fat 4.5g (Saturated Fat 1g, Trans Fat 0g); Cholesterol 100mg; Sodium 670mg; Total Carbohydrate 35g (Dietary Fiber 2g); Protein 22g **Exchanges:** 2 Starch, ½ Vegetable, 2 Very Lean Meat, ½ Fat **Carbohydrate Choices:** 2

> TIME-SAVER Keep extra cooked chicken stored in your freezer to thaw and use for recipes like this one. Or, purchase a rotisserie chicken from the deli and cut up what you need.

Crusty French bread slices served with olive oil for dipping are the perfect go-with for this hearty soup.

Prep Time:
30 Minutes

Start to Finish:
30 Minutes

6 servings
(1½ cups each)

Italian Chicken Noodle Soup

1	tablespoon olive or vegetable oil	3	medium carrots, sliced (1½ cups)
½	lb boneless skinless chicken breasts, cut into ½-inch pieces	2	cups small fresh broccoli florets
1	medium onion, chopped (½ cup)	1½	cups uncooked egg noodles (3 oz)
1	carton (32 oz) chicken broth (4 cups)	1	teaspoon dried basil leaves
2	cups water	½	teaspoon garlic-pepper blend
		¼	cup shredded Parmesan cheese (1 oz)

1 In 4-quart Dutch oven or saucepan, heat oil over medium heat. Cook chicken in oil 4 to 6 minutes, stirring occasionally, until no longer pink in center. Add onion. Cook 2 to 3 minutes, stirring occasionally, until onion is tender.

2 Stir in broth, water and carrots. Heat to boiling over medium heat. Cook 5 minutes. Stir in broccoli, noodles, basil and garlic-pepper blend. Heat to boiling; reduce heat. Simmer uncovered 8 to 10 minutes, stirring occasionally, until vegetables and noodles are tender. Top individual servings with cheese.

1 Serving: Calories 170; Total Fat 6g (Saturated Fat 2g, Trans Fat 0g); Cholesterol 35mg; Sodium 710mg; Total Carbohydrate 13g (Dietary Fiber 2g); Protein 15g **Exchanges:** 1 Starch, 1½ Very Lean Meat, 1 Fat **Carbohydrate Choices:** 1

> TRY THIS You can substitute chicken thighs for part or all of the chicken breasts. And you can use frozen carrots and broccoli instead of fresh, if you like.

You won't miss the fat or calories taken out of this favorite soup, and you'll love the extra vitamin A from red peppers and baby spinach!

Thai Chicken Soup

Prep Time:
30 Minutes

Start to Finish:
30 Minutes

6 servings
(about 1 cup each)

1	teaspoon canola oil	1½	cups shredded cooked chicken breast
1	small onion, cut into thin wedges (1 cup)	1	teaspoon packed brown sugar
2	cups sliced fresh mushrooms (6 oz)	¼	teaspoon salt
½	medium red bell pepper, cut into thin bite-size strips (1 cup)	1	tablespoon cornstarch
2	cloves garlic, finely chopped	2	tablespoons cold water
1	teaspoon red curry paste	1	can (14 oz) reduced-fat (lite) coconut milk (not cream of coconut)
1	carton (32 oz) reduced-sodium chicken broth (4 cups)	4	cups fresh baby spinach leaves
		2	tablespoons chopped fresh cilantro
			Lime wedges, if desired

1 In 4-quart nonstick Dutch oven, heat oil over medium heat. Add onion and mushrooms; cook 3 minutes, stirring frequently. Add bell pepper and garlic; cook 2 to 3 minutes longer, stirring frequently, until vegetables are tender. Remove from heat; stir in curry paste until melted.

2 Stir in broth, chicken, brown sugar and salt. Return to heat. Heat to boiling. Reduce heat; simmer uncovered 5 minutes, stirring frequently.

3 In small bowl, stir cornstarch and water until smooth. Add cornstarch mixture and coconut milk to soup mixture; heat to boiling. Cook over medium heat about 2 minutes, stirring frequently, until slightly thickened.

4 Stir in spinach and cilantro. Cook about 1 minute or just until mixture is hot and spinach is wilted. Serve soup with lime wedges.

1 Serving: Calories 150 (Calories from Fat 60); Total Fat 7g (Saturated Fat 4g, Trans Fat 0g); Cholesterol 30mg; Sodium 550mg; Total Carbohydrate 8g (Dietary Fiber 1g, Sugars 4g); Protein 14g **Exchanges:** ½ Other Carbohydrate, 2 Lean Meat **Carbohydrate Choices:** ½

A fun take on classic chicken noodle soup! You and your family will love the twist of turkey and the unusual spaetzle noodles for a quick meal that satisfies on a blustery day.

Prep Time:
25 Minutes

Start to Finish:
25 Minutes

6 servings

Turkey-Spaetzle Soup

2   **tablespoons vegetable oil**

1   **large onion, finely chopped (1 cup)**

1   **medium carrot, finely chopped (½ cup)**

1   **medium stalk celery, finely chopped (½ cup)**

1   **clove garlic, finely chopped**

¼   **cup all-purpose flour**

1   **tablespoon chopped fresh or 2 teaspoons dried thyme leaves**

¼   **teaspoon pepper**

2   **cups diced cooked turkey**

6   **cups chicken broth (from two 32-oz cartons)**

1   **bag (12 oz) frozen spaetzle**

Chopped fresh parsley, if desired

1 In 4-quart Dutch oven or saucepan, heat oil over medium-high heat. Cook onion, carrot, celery and garlic in oil about 2 minutes, stirring frequently, until crisp-tender.

2 Gradually stir in flour, thyme and pepper; cook 1 minute, stirring constantly. Stir in turkey and broth; heat to boiling.

3 Stir in frozen spaetzle. Cook 2 to 3 minutes, stirring occasionally, until spaetzle are tender. Sprinkle with parsley.

1 Serving: Calories 240; Total Fat 10g (Saturated Fat 2.5g, Trans Fat 0g); Cholesterol 70mg; Sodium 1180mg; Total Carbohydrate 17g (Dietary Fiber 2g); Protein 21g **Exchanges:** 1 Starch, 2½ Lean Meat, ½ Fat **Carbohydrate Choices:** 1

> TRY THIS If you prefer, substitute 3 cups frozen egg noodles (from a 16-ounce bag) for the spaetzle.

Prep Time:
30 Minutes

Start to Finish:
30 Minutes

6 servings
(1½ cups each)

Frozen vegetables are great to keep on hand. They are easy, won't go limp in the crisper and retain the vitamins and nutrients that they had when picked. Recipes like this easy soup take advantage of their convenience.

Easy Vegetable-Beef Soup

SEASONING BLEND

1	cup chopped onion (1 large)
4½	teaspoons finely chopped garlic
1	teaspoon Italian seasoning
½	teaspoon pepper
¼	teaspoon salt

SOUP

1	lb lean (at least 80%) ground beef
2½	cups water
1	bag (16 oz) frozen mixed vegetables, thawed
1	can (14.5 oz) Italian-style stewed tomatoes, undrained, chopped
1	can (8 oz) tomato sauce

1 In small bowl, mix seasoning blend ingredients.

2 In 4-quart Dutch oven or saucepan, cook beef and seasoning blend over medium-high heat 5 to 7 minutes, stirring occasionally, until beef is thoroughly cooked; drain.

3 Stir in remaining soup ingredients. Heat to boiling over medium-high heat; reduce heat. Cover; simmer 15 minutes, stirring occasionally, until hot.

1 Serving: Calories 210; Total Fat 9g (Saturated Fat 3.5g, Trans Fat 0.5g); Cholesterol 45mg; Sodium 730mg; Total Carbohydrate 16g (Dietary Fiber 4g); Protein 16g **Exchanges:** ½ Other Carbohydrate, 1 Vegetable, 2 Medium-Fat Meat **Carbohydrate Choices:** 1

Angel hair pasta cooks in a flash and is a great alternative to thicker noodles. In this soup, pasta is a great foil for the complex, spicy flavor lent by the Sriracha sauce.

Prep Time:
25 Minutes

Start to Finish:
25 Minutes

6 servings (about 1⅓ cups each)

Spicy Angel Hair Pasta and Meatball Soup

1 **tablespoon olive oil**	1 **tablespoon Sriracha sauce**
1 **medium onion, chopped (½ cup)**	½ **teaspoon garlic salt**
3 **cans (14.5 oz each) diced tomatoes with Italian-style herbs, undrained**	4 **oz uncooked angel hair (cappellini) pasta, broken into 2-inch pieces**
3½ **cups chicken broth (from 32-oz carton)**	24 **frozen cooked Italian-style meatballs (from 16-oz bag)**

1 In 5-quart Dutch oven or stockpot, heat oil over medium-high heat. Cook onion in oil about 3 minutes, stirring occasionally, until tender. Stir in tomatoes, broth, Sriracha sauce and garlic salt. Heat to boiling, stirring occasionally.

2 Stir in pasta and meatballs. Heat to boiling; reduce heat. Cover; simmer about 6 minutes, stirring occasionally, until pasta is tender and meatballs are thoroughly heated.

1 Serving: Calories 460; Total Fat 19g (Saturated Fat 6g, Trans Fat 1g); Cholesterol 120mg; Sodium 1810mg; Total Carbohydrate 41g (Dietary Fiber 4g); Protein 30g **Exchanges:** 2 Starch, ½ Other Carbohydrate, 2 Lean Meat, 1½ Medium-Fat Meat, 1 Fat **Carbohydrate Choices:** 3

There's no reason to choose between white or sweet potatoes! The two complement each other beautifully in this delicious and hearty chowder.

Prep Time:
30 Minutes

Start to Finish:
30 Minutes

5 servings
(1¼ cups each)

Two-Potato Ham Chowder

½ cup chopped leek or onion

2 cups reduced-sodium chicken broth (from 32-oz carton)

2 medium baking potatoes, peeled, each cut into 6 pieces

2 cups cubed (½ inch) peeled dark-orange sweet potatoes (about 2 medium)

1 cup diced cooked ham

1 cup frozen sweet peas

2 tablespoons chopped fresh chives

½ teaspoon salt

¼ teaspoon pepper

1 cup half-and-half or milk

1 Spray 3-quart saucepan with cooking spray; heat over medium heat. Add leek; cook 3 minutes, stirring frequently, until softened. Increase heat to high. Add broth and baking potatoes. Heat to boiling; reduce heat. Cover; simmer 5 minutes.

2 Add sweet potatoes. Cover; simmer about 10 minutes or until potatoes are tender when pierced with fork.

3 Using slotted spoon, transfer baking potatoes to blender. With lid on saucepan, carefully drain broth into blender, leaving leek and sweet potatoes in pan. Cover blender; puree potato mixture until smooth. Return mixture to saucepan.

4 Stir in remaining ingredients. Cook over medium heat about 8 minutes, stirring occasionally, until thoroughly heated.

1 Serving: Calories 240; Total Fat 8g (Saturated Fat 4.5g, Trans Fat 0g); Cholesterol 35mg; Sodium 900mg; Total Carbohydrate 28g (Dietary Fiber 4g); Protein 12g **Exchanges:** 1½ Starch, 1 Vegetable, ½ Very Lean Meat, ½ Lean Meat, 1 Fat **Carbohydrate Choices:** 2

> TIME-SAVER Look for packages of diced cooked ham near the refrigerated deli meats and bacon at the grocery store.

Feeling spicy? Choose how much you want to amp up the bite in this simple soup based on the sausage you choose.

Prep Time:
25 Minutes

Start to Finish:
25 Minutes

4 servings

Italian Sausage and Pepper Stew

1   package (19.5 oz) Italian turkey
    sausage (sweet or hot), casings
    removed, links cut into 2-inch pieces

1   large red bell pepper, cut into
    bite-size strips

1   large yellow bell pepper, cut into
    bite-size strips

1   can (14.5 oz) diced tomatoes,
    undrained

1   teaspoon dried basil leaves, crushed

2⅔ cups uncooked penne rigate pasta
    (8 oz)

    Grated Parmesan cheese, if desired

1 In 4-quart Dutch oven or saucepan, cook sausage and bell peppers over medium-high heat, about 8 minutes, stirring occasionally, until sausage is no longer pink; drain.

2 Reduce heat to medium-low. Stir in tomatoes and basil. Cover; simmer 10 minutes.

3 Meanwhile, cook and drain pasta as directed on package. Serve sausage and peppers over pasta; sprinkle with cheese.

1 Serving: Calories 550; Total Fat 16g (Saturated Fat 3.5g, Trans Fat 0.5g); Cholesterol 125mg; Sodium 1070mg; Total Carbohydrate 58g (Dietary Fiber 5g); Protein 43g **Exchanges:** 3½ Starch, 1 Vegetable, 4½ Lean Meat **Carbohydrate Choices:** 4

Enjoy this Asian-style soup made with pork, egg noodles and vegetables for a delightful and flavorful meal!

Prep Time:
30 Minutes

Start to Finish:
30 Minutes

5 servings

Asian Pork and Noodle Soup

1	lb boneless pork loin, cut into ½-inch pieces	2	tablespoons soy sauce
2	cloves garlic, finely chopped	2	cups uncooked fine egg noodles (4 oz)
2	teaspoons finely chopped gingerroot	1	medium carrot, sliced (½ cup)
3½	cups chicken broth (from 32-oz carton)	1	small red bell pepper, chopped (½ cup)
2	cups water	2	cups fresh spinach leaves

1 Spray 3-quart saucepan with cooking spray; heat over medium-high heat. Add pork, garlic and gingerroot; cook 3 to 5 minutes, stirring frequently, until pork is brown.

2 Stir in broth, water and soy sauce. Heat to boiling. Reduce heat; simmer uncovered 5 minutes.

3 Stir in noodles. carrot and bell pepper. Simmer uncovered about 10 minutes, stirring occasionally, until noodles are tender and pork is no longer pink in the center. Stir in spinach; cook until hot.

1 Serving: Calories 230 (Calories from Fat 50); Total Fat 6g (Saturated Fat 2g, Trans Fat 0g); Sodium 1140mg; Total Carbohydrate 19g (Dietary Fiber 1g); Protein 25g **Exchanges:** 1 Starch, ½ Vegetable, 3 Very Lean Meat, 1 Fat **Carbohydrate Choices:** 1

15 MINUTES OR LESS

Some on-hand pantry and freezer ingredients come together quickly for a home-cooked dinner perfect for even the busiest of nights.

Prep Time:
15 Minutes

Start to Finish:
15 Minutes

4 servings

Speedy Cassoulet

1   can (15 to 16 oz) cannellini or great northern beans, drained, rinsed

1   can (14.5 oz) diced tomatoes with roasted garlic (or other variety), undrained

1   can (14 oz) chicken broth

½   lb cooked turkey kielbasa, cut into ½-inch slices

1½   cups frozen chopped green bell pepper (from 10-oz bag), thawed

Seasoned bread crumbs, if desired

> TRY THIS You can substitute 1½ cups frozen bell pepper and onion stir-fry (from 1-lb bag) for the green bell pepper.

1 In 3-quart saucepan, heat beans, tomatoes, broth and kielbasa to boiling, stirring occasionally; reduce heat.

2 Stir in bell pepper. Simmer uncovered 5 minutes, stirring occasionally, until thoroughly heated. Sprinkle individual servings with bread crumbs.

1 Serving: Calories 290; Total Fat 6g (Saturated Fat 1.5g, Trans Fat 0g); Cholesterol 30mg; Sodium 1170mg; Total Carbohydrate 35g (Dietary Fiber 9g); Protein 22g **Exchanges:** 2 Starch, 1 Vegetable, 2 Very Lean Meat **Carbohydrate Choices:** 2

Have dinner on the Bayou—or at least feel like it!— with this pork and shrimp-filled soup, a Louisiana classic.

Prep Time:
30 Minutes

Start to Finish:
30 Minutes

5 servings
(1½ cups each)

Home-Style Gumbo

1	tablespoon vegetable oil		½	teaspoon dried thyme leaves
1	cup chopped onion		½	teaspoon dried basil leaves
1	cup chopped celery		½	to 1 teaspoon hot pepper sauce
1	medium green bell pepper, chopped		1	can (14.5 oz) diced tomatoes, undrained
2	cloves garlic, finely chopped		1	cup uncooked instant white rice
½	lb boneless pork loin, cut into thin strips		1	bag (12 oz) frozen cooked deveined peeled shrimp, thawed
2½	cups chicken broth (from 32-oz carton)			

> GO-WITH IDEA
Hot cornbread and iced tea are perfect accompaniments to this Southern-inspired gumbo. For dessert, serve another Southern specialty—pecan pie or pecan cookies.

1 In 4-quart Dutch oven or saucepan, heat oil over medium-high heat. Cook onion, celery, bell pepper and garlic in oil 5 minutes, stirring occasionally, until tender. Add pork; cook 2 to 3 minutes or until no longer pink.

2 Stir in broth, thyme, basil, pepper sauce and tomatoes. Heat to boiling. Stir in rice and shrimp. Remove from heat; cover and let stand 5 minutes or until rice is tender and shrimp are hot. Serve with additional pepper sauce, if desired.

1 Serving Calories 280; Total Fat 8g (Saturated Fat 2g, Trans Fat 0g); Cholesterol 135mg; Sodium 1070mg; Total Carbohydrate 27g (Dietary Fiber 2g); Protein 25g **Exchanges:** 1 Starch, ½ Other Carbohydrate, ½ Vegetable, 3 Very Lean Meat, 1 Fat **Carbohydrate Choices:** 2

Looking for a light lunch or supper? Try this elegant entrée, which is perfect for a warm summer evening. Add a mesclun salad with a light vinaigrette for a complete, but still light, meal.

Prep Time:
25 Minutes

Start to Finish:
25 Minutes

8 servings
(1 cup each)

Provençal Fish Soup

1	**tablespoon olive oil**
1	**medium onion, chopped (½ cup)**
1	**carton (32 oz) chicken broth (4 cups)**
2	**cans (14.5 oz each) diced tomatoes with basil, garlic and oregano, undrained**

½	**cup dry white wine or dry vermouth**
¼	**teaspoon pepper**
1	**lb halibut fillet, skinned, cut into 1-inch cubes**
	Toasted baguette slices, shaved Parmesan cheese and chopped fresh parsley, if desired

1 In 3-quart saucepan, heat oil over medium heat. Cook onion in oil 2 to 3 minutes, stirring occasionally, until crisp-tender.

2 Add broth, tomatoes, wine and pepper. Heat to boiling; reduce heat. Simmer uncovered 10 minutes, stirring occasionally.

3 Stir in fish. Heat to boiling; reduce heat. Simmer 5 minutes or until fish flakes easily with fork. Serve in shallow bowls topped with baguette slices and cheese; sprinkle with parsley.

1 Serving: Calories 100; Total Fat 2.5g (Saturated Fat 0g, Trans Fat 0g); Cholesterol 25mg; Sodium 640mg; Total Carbohydrate 6g (Dietary Fiber 1g); Protein 11g **Exchanges:** ½ Other Carbohydrate, 1½ Very Lean Meat, ½ Fat **Carbohydrate Choices:** ½

> TRY THIS Cod or grouper can be substituted for the halibut.

20 MINUTES OR LESS

Prep Time:
20 Minutes

Start to Finish:
20 Minutes

10 servings
(1 cup each)

Last-minute guests? Rely on this upscale French dinner that is ready in 20 minutes! Crab and oyster come together in a flavorful bisque that tastes like you slaved over the stove.

Crab and Oyster Bisque

¼ cup butter	¼ teaspoon pepper
4 cloves garlic, finely chopped	1 quart (4 cups) whipping cream
2 shallots, finely chopped	1 container (12 oz) fresh oysters, drained
3 tablespoons all-purpose flour	1 lb fresh lump crabmeat
1 bottle (8 oz) clam juice	Oyster crackers, if desired
1 cup dry white wine	Chopped fresh Italian (flat-leaf) parsley
1 tablespoon Worchestershire sauce	
1 teaspoon Cajun seasoning	

1 In a 4- to 5-quart Dutch over or stockpot, melt butter over medium heat. Cook garlic and shallots in butter, stirring occasionally, until tender. Add flour; cook 1 minute, stirring constantly. Add clam juice and wine; cook 2 minutes, stirring constantly, until thickened.

2 Stir in Worcestershire sauce, Cajun seasoning, pepper and whipping cream. Cook until thoroughly heated, about 10 minutes. Stir in oysters and crabmeat; cook just until edges of oysters curl. Serve with oyster crackers; sprinkle with parsley.

1 Serving: Calories 362; Total Fat 35g (Saturated Fat 22g, Trans Fat nc); Sodium 219mg; Total Carbohydrate 7g (Dietary Fiber 0g); Protein 4g **Exchanges:** ½ Starch, ½ Very Lean Meat, 7 Fat **Carbohydrate Choices:** ½

> TRY THIS 1 medium chopped tomato and 1 medium shredded carrot added with the oysters will add color while also balancing the rich flavor of this soup.

Prep Time:
30 Minutes

Start to Finish:
30 Minutes

5 servings
(1½ cups each)

Fire-roasted tomatoes have a depth of flavor that can elevate even simple dishes. Keep several cans on hand in the pantry and you'll always be able to make simple foods with complex flavors, like this Italian-inspired soup.

Fire-Roasted Tomato Basil Soup

1	tablespoon olive or vegetable oil		1	carton (32 oz) chicken broth (4 cups)
1	large onion, chopped (1 cup)		1	cup water
2	medium carrots, chopped (1 cup)		1	teaspoon red pepper sauce
2	cans (14.5 oz each) fire-roasted diced tomatoes, undrained		½	cup uncooked orzo pasta (3 oz)
			1	teaspoon dried basil leaves

1 In 4-quart Dutch oven or saucepan, heat oil over medium heat. Cook onion and carrots in oil 2 to 3 minutes, stirring occasionally, until softened.

2 Stir in tomatoes, broth, water and pepper sauce. Heat to boiling. Stir in pasta. Return to boiling; reduce heat to medium. Cook uncovered 10 to 15 minutes, stirring occasionally, until pasta and carrots are tender.

3 Stir in basil. Cook about 1 minute, stirring constantly.

1 Serving: Calories 160; Total Fat 4g (Saturated Fat 0.5g, Trans Fat 0g); Cholesterol 0mg; Sodium 990mg; Total Carbohydrate 23g (Dietary Fiber 4g); Protein 7g **Exchanges:** 1½ Starch, 1 Vegetable, ½ Fat **Carbohydrate Choices:** 1½

> GO-WITH IDEA This slightly smoky-flavored soup is delicious served with grilled cheese sandwiches.

If you don't have kidney beans on hand, try another type of beans in this versatile soup, such as black or cannellini. And to amp up the green quotient, substitute spinach and cheese-filled ravioli for the cheese-filled ravioli.

Tortellini and Bean Soup

Prep Time:
20 Minutes

Start to Finish:
20 Minutes

4 servings
(1¼ cups each)

3½ cups water	1 cup frozen cut leaf spinach
2 vegetable bouillon cubes	1 can (15 oz) red kidney beans, drained, rinsed
1 can (14.5 oz) diced tomatoes with basil, garlic and oregano, undrained	1 package (9 oz) refrigerated cheese-filled tortellini

1 In 3-quart saucepan, heat water, bouillon and tomatoes to boiling over medium-high heat.

2 Stir in spinach, beans and tortellini. Return to boiling; reduce heat. Cook 5 minutes, stirring occasionally, until thoroughly heated and tortellini is tender.

> GO-WITH IDEA
Complete the meal with a crusty French baguette and a mixed-green salad topped with pistachios and tossed with a zesty vinaigrette.

1 Serving: Calories 330; Total Fat 5g (Saturated Fat 2.5g, Trans Fat 0g); Cholesterol 20mg; Sodium 1250mg; Total Carbohydrate 53g (Dietary Fiber 8g); Protein 17g **Exchanges:** 1½ Starch, 2 Other Carbohydrate, ½ Vegetable, 1½ Very Lean Meat, ½ Fat **Carbohydrate Choices:** 3½

Cauliflower

There's no limit to the number of ways cauliflower can be prepared. With its raw, crunchy texture and neutral flavor, it's a natural to combine with a wide range of ingredients. It pairs especially well with cheeses such as Cheddar and Parmesan and a variety of other vegetables.

This popular vegetable is available year-round, but peak growing season is typically early summer into fall. Purchase cauliflower heads that are tight and firm and avoid any with discoloration. To use, trim away the leaves and stem end before cutting. To store, keep in the coldest part of your refrigerator for four to seven days.

Here are some delicious ways to use fresh cauliflower.

CAULIFLOWER STEAKS WITH FIRE-ROASTED TOMATOES Cut cauliflower into 1-inch slices to make cauliflower steaks. In 10-inch skillet, cook steaks in 1 to 2 tablespoons olive oil until light golden brown but still firm. Place steaks on individual serving plates. Spoon about ¼ cup heated fire-roasted diced tomatoes over each serving. Sprinkle with chopped fresh oregano and shredded Asiago cheese.

CRUNCHY RANCH CAULIFLOWER SALAD In large bowl, stir ½ cup ranch dressing, 1 head cauliflower separated into small florets, ½ cup chopped bell pepper, 4 ounces diced Colby cheese and ½ cup chopped, cooked bacon.

ROASTED CAULIFLOWER WITH PARMESAN Place 3 cups cauliflower florets on lightly greased 15x10x1-inch pan. Toss with 2 tablespoons olive oil, 2 cloves chopped garlic, ¼ teaspoon salt and ½ teaspoon paprika. Bake at 425°F for 15 to 20 minutes or just until fork-tender. Sprinkle with ¼ cup shredded fresh Parmesan cheese.

CAULIFLOWER CAESAR SALAD In large bowl, toss 2 cups small cauliflower florets with 4 cups (1 bag) Caesar salad mix and ¼ to ½ cup Caesar salad dressing. Sprinkle with garlic croutons and shredded fresh Parmesan cheese.

CAULIFLOWER WITH TOMATOES AND PARSLEY In microwavable bowl, cook 2 to 3 cups cauliflower florets in microwave on High for 4 to 6 minutes or just until tender, stirring once or twice. Add 1 cup halved cherry tomatoes and ¼ cup chopped fresh parsley. Sprinkle with salt and pepper to taste.

ITALIAN CAULIFLOWER WITH BROCCOLI In large bowl, toss 2 cups each hot, cooked cauliflower florets and broccoli florets with ½ cup Italian dressing and 2 tablespoons pine nuts.

The flavor of cauliflower is intensified through roasting in this complex soup that also stars the creaminess of cheese and salty bite of bacon. Thyme leaves add a freshness to the creamy soup.

Prep Time:
30 Minutes

Start to Finish:
30 Minutes

4 servings
(1¼ cups each)

Pan-Roasted Cauliflower Soup

1	**medium head cauliflower (1½ lb), separated into florets**
3	**tablespoons olive oil**
2	**cups chicken broth**
1½	**cups half-and-half**
1½	**teaspoons chopped fresh thyme leaves**

¾	**teaspoon salt**
1½	**cups shredded Cheddar cheese (6 oz)**
4	**slices bacon, crisply cooked, crumbled**
	Additional shredded Cheddar cheese, if desired
	Fresh thyme sprigs, if desired

1 Pat cauliflower dry with paper towels so it will brown more quickly and easily. Coarsely chop into ½-inch pieces (about 6 cups). In 12-inch skillet, heat oil over medium heat. Spread cauliflower in single layer in skillet. Cook 8 to 10 minutes, stirring occasionally, until golden brown.

2 Stir in broth, half-and-half, chopped thyme and salt. Heat to boiling; reduce heat. Simmer 5 minutes, stirring occasionally, until cauliflower is tender. Remove from heat; stir in cheese until melted.

3 Carefully pour 3 cups of the soup into blender (making sure to get equal amounts of cauliflower and broth). Cover; blend on medium speed about 30 to 45 seconds, stopping blender occasionally to scrape sides, until smooth. Return to skillet with remaining soup; stir to blend. Heat just until hot, if necessary.

4 Garnish individual servings with bacon, additional cheese and thyme sprigs.

1 Serving: Calories 470; Total Fat 38g (Saturated Fat 18g, Trans Fat 0.5g); Cholesterol 85mg; Sodium 1380mg; Total Carbohydrate 12g (Dietary Fiber 3g); Protein 19g **Exchanges:** 2½ Vegetable, 2 High-Fat Meat, 4½ Fat **Carbohydrate Choices:** 1

Jarred basil pesto is a great pantry item to keep on hand for lending complex flavor to soups, stews and sandwiches. Here it elevates a simple soup to a more nuanced and flavorful meal.

Prep Time:
15 Minutes

Start to Finish:
15 Minutes

4 servings

Italian Tomato Soup with Pesto-Cheese Toasts

1 **cup water**	4 **slices (½ inch thick) rosemary, Italian or French bread**
2 **cans (14.5 oz each) diced tomatoes with Italian-style herbs, undrained**	2 **tablespoons basil pesto**
1 **can (11.5 oz) tomato juice**	2 **tablespoons shredded Parmesan cheese**

1 In 3-quart saucepan, heat water, tomatoes and tomato juice to boiling.

2 Meanwhile, set oven control to broil. Spread each slice of bread with pesto; sprinkle evenly with cheese. Place bread on cookie sheet. Broil with tops 4 to 6 inches from heat 1 to 2 minutes or until edges are golden brown.

3 Ladle soup into 4 bowls; top each with bread slice.

1 Serving: Calories 260; Total Fat 7g (Saturated Fat 2g, Trans Fat 0g); Cholesterol 0mg; Sodium 910mg; Total Carbohydrate 39g (Dietary Fiber 4g); Protein 9g **Exchanges:** 1½ Starch, ½ Other Carbohydrate, 2 Vegetable, 1½ Fat **Carbohydrate Choices:** 2½

A nice spin on classic red chili, this Mexican staple features tomatillo salsa (also called salsa verde) for a fun twist. If you like, sprinkle some Mexican-blend cheese on top of each serving.

Prep Time:
15 Minutes

Start to Finish:
15 Minutes

4 servings
(1½ cups each)

Tortilla Green Chili

1   can (15 oz) black beans with cumin and chili, undrained

1   can (14.5 oz) diced tomatoes with green chiles, undrained

1   bag (12 oz) frozen whole kernel corn

1   jar (16 oz) mild green tomatillo salsa

½   cup coarsely crushed tortilla chips (about 1 oz)

1   avocado, pitted, peeled and cut into cubes

1   lime, sliced, then cut into quarters

¼   cup sour cream

1   In 3-quart saucepan, stir together beans, tomatoes, corn, salsa and tortilla chips. Heat to boiling; reduce heat to medium.

2   Cover; simmer 5 to 10 minutes, stirring occasionally, until slightly thickened. Top individual servings with avocado, lime, sour cream and, if desired, additional tortilla chips.

1 Serving: Calories 390; Total Fat 13g (Saturated Fat 3g, Trans Fat 0g); Cholesterol 10mg; Sodium 940mg; Total Carbohydrate 56g (Dietary Fiber 14g); Protein 12g **Exchanges:** 2 Starch, ½ Fruit, ½ Other Carbohydrate, 1½ Vegetable, ½ Very Lean Meat, 2½ Fat **Carbohydrate Choices:** 4

CHAPTER 3

Stovetop and Roasted Foods

Asparagus is at the peak of freshness in March and April, which is a wonderful time to enjoy this flavorful meal.

Prep Time:
30 Minutes

Start to Finish:
30 Minutes

4 servings

Honey-Dijon Turkey Tenderloins and Asparagus

1 package (20 oz) turkey breast tenderloins, cut into ½-inch-thick slices	2 tablespoons coarse-grained Dijon mustard
1 teaspoon dried thyme leaves	1 tablespoon honey
¾ teaspoon garlic-pepper blend	1 tablespoon cornstarch
2 tablespoons olive oil	1 lb fresh asparagus, trimmed, cut into 2-inch pieces (3 cups)
1 cup chicken broth	1½ cups grape tomatoes, cut in half

1 Sprinkle turkey with thyme and garlic-pepper blend. In 12-inch skillet, heat 1 tablespoon of the oil over medium-high heat. Cook turkey in oil 5 to 7 minutes, turning once, until juice of turkey is clear when center of thickest part is cut (at least 165°F). Remove from skillet; cover to keep warm.

2 In small bowl, mix broth, mustard, honey and cornstarch; set aside.

3 In same skillet, heat remaining 1 tablespoon oil over medium-high heat. Cook asparagus in oil 3 minutes, stirring frequently. Add turkey and broth mixture. Cook 1 minute, stirring constantly, until sauce is thickened. Add tomatoes; cook 1 minute longer, stirring constantly.

1 Serving: Calories 290; Total Fat 9g (Saturated Fat 1.5g, Trans Fat 0g); Cholesterol 95mg; Sodium 590mg; Total Carbohydrate 14g (Dietary Fiber 3g); Protein 37g **Exchanges:** ½ Other Carbohydrate, 2 Vegetable, 2 Very Lean Meat, 2½ Lean Meat **Carbohydrate Choices:** 1

This easy one-pot dinner is ready in under 30 minutes and bursting with clean, fresh ingredients.

Prep Time:
15 Minutes

Start to Finish:
25 Minutes

4 servings
(1½ cups each)

Pan-Roasted Chicken and Cauliflower

1	tablespoon olive oil
2	cups small fresh cauliflower florets
1½	cups chicken broth
1¼	lb boneless skinless chicken thighs, cut into bite-size pieces
1	cup uncooked orzo pasta (6 oz)

¼	cup thinly sliced green onions (4 medium)
1	can (14.5 oz) diced tomatoes with basil, garlic and oregano, drained
2	cups packed arugula or fresh baby spinach leaves
½	cup shredded Parmesan cheese (2 oz)

1 In 12-inch nonstick skillet, heat oil over medium heat. Cook cauliflower in oil about 5 minutes, stirring occasionally, until lightly browned.

2 Stir in broth, chicken, pasta, onions and tomatoes. Heat to boiling; reduce heat. Cover; simmer 8 to 10 minutes or until chicken is no longer pink in center and pasta is tender.

3 Remove from heat. Stir in arugula. Cover; let stand about 1 minute or until arugula is partially wilted. Sprinkle with cheese.

1 Serving: Calories 380; Total Fat 14g (Saturated Fat 5g, Trans Fat 0g); Cholesterol 55mg; Sodium 780mg; Total Carbohydrate 35g (Dietary Fiber 3g); Protein 28g **Exchanges:** 1½ Starch, 2 Vegetable, ½ Lean Meat, 2½ Medium-Fat Meat **Carbohydrate Choices:** 2

Chicken curry is a flavorful favorite that comes together quickly in this delicious stir-fry. Serve over rice for a complete family meal.

Prep Time:
15 Minutes

Start to Finish:
25 Minutes

4 servings

Coconut-Curry Chicken

1	tablespoon curry powder
¾	lb boneless skinless chicken breasts
1	teaspoon vegetable oil
1	small onion, cut into thin wedges
1	small zucchini, cut into ¼-inch slices
1	medium bell pepper (any color), cut into ¾-inch pieces

⅓	cup reduced-fat (lite) unsweetened coconut milk (not cream of coconut)
1	tablespoon brown bean sauce
1	teaspoon grated gingerroot
½	teaspoon salt
2	tablespoons shredded coconut, toasted*

1 Rub curry powder on chicken. Cut chicken into ¾-inch pieces. Let stand 10 minutes.

2 Spray wok or 12-inch skillet with cooking spray; heat over medium-high heat until cooking spray starts to bubble. Add chicken; cook 2 minutes, stirring constantly, until no longer pink in center. Move chicken to side of wok.

3 Add oil to center of wok. Add onion, zucchini and bell pepper; cook 2 minutes, stirring constantly. Add coconut milk, bean sauce, gingerroot and salt; cook and stir until sauce coats vegetables and chicken is hot. Sprinkle with toasted coconut.

*To toast coconut, sprinkle in ungreased skillet. Cook over medium-low heat 6 to 14 minutes, stirring frequently until browning begins, then stirring constantly until golden brown.

1 Serving: Calories 170; Total Fat 6g (Saturated Fat 3g, Trans Fat 0g); Cholesterol 55mg; Sodium 400mg; Total Carbohydrate 8g (Dietary Fiber 2g); Protein 20g **Exchanges:** 1 Vegetable, 2½ Lean Meat **Carbohydrate Choices:** ½

The flavors of a classic Italian caprese salad—tomato, basil and mozzarella—are upgraded to a full meal served over (what else?) pasta.

Caprese Chicken

4	**boneless skinless chicken breasts (1 to 1¼ lb)**
1	**teaspoon Italian seasoning**
½	**teaspoon salt**
½	**teaspoon grated lemon peel**
1	**tablespoon olive oil**
1	**teaspoon balsamic vinegar**
1	**large plum (Roma) tomato, cut into 8 thin slices**
½	**cup shredded mozzarella cheese (2 oz)**
¼	**cup chopped fresh basil leaves**
	Hot, cooked linguine, if desired

1 Between pieces of plastic wrap or waxed paper, place each chicken breast smooth side down; gently pound with flat side of meat mallet or rolling pin until about ½ inch thick. In small bowl, mix Italian seasoning, salt and lemon peel; rub mixture evenly over smooth side of chicken.

2 In 10-inch nonstick skillet, heat oil and vinegar over medium-high heat. Add chicken, seasoned side down; cook 8 to 10 minutes, turning once, until no longer pink in center.

3 Reduce heat to low. Top each chicken breast with 2 tomato slices and 2 tablespoons cheese. Cover; cook 2 minutes or until cheese is melted. Sprinkle with basil. Serve with linguine.

1 Serving: Calories 250; Total Fat 11g (Saturated Fat 4g, Trans Fat 0g); Cholesterol 95mg; Sodium 460mg; Total Carbohydrate 2g (Dietary Fiber 0g); Protein 36g **Exchanges:** 4 Very Lean Meat, ½ Lean Meat, ½ Medium-Fat Meat, 1 Fat **Carbohydrate Choices:** 0

30 MINUTES OR LESS

Prep Time:
30 Minutes

Start to Finish:
30 Minutes

2 servings

Orzo (rice-shaped pasta) is a versatile pantry item that can complement many meals. Here it's the perfect companion for chicken infused with rosemary. While dried rosemary will work just fine for this recipe, if you really want to intensify the flavor, go for fresh.

Mediterranean Chicken with Rosemary Orzo

½ lb uncooked chicken breast tenders (not breaded)

1 clove garlic, finely chopped

¾ cup uncooked orzo pasta (4½ oz)

1 cup chicken broth

¼ cup water

2 teaspoons chopped fresh or ½ teaspoon dried rosemary leaves

¼ teaspoon salt

1 medium zucchini, cut lengthwise into fourths, then cut crosswise into slices (¾ cup)

2 plum (Roma) tomatoes, cut into fourths and sliced (1 cup)

½ medium bell pepper (any color), chopped (½ cup)

1 Heat 10-inch nonstick skillet over medium-high heat. Add chicken; cook about 5 minutes, stirring frequently, until golden brown.

2 Stir in garlic, pasta and broth. Heat to boiling; reduce heat. Cover; simmer about 8 minutes or until most of liquid is absorbed.

3 Stir in remaining ingredients. Heat to boiling; reduce heat. Cover; simmer about 5 minutes, stirring once, until bell pepper is crisp-tender and pasta is tender.

1 Serving: Calories 370; Total Fat 6g (Saturated Fat 1.5g, Trans Fat 0g); Cholesterol 70mg; Sodium 880mg; Total Carbohydrate 47g (Dietary Fiber 5g); Protein 35g **Exchanges:** 2 Starch, ½ Other Carbohydrate, 2 Vegetable, 3½ Very Lean Meat, ½ Fat **Carbohydrate Choices:** 3

> TRY THIS This is a delicious meal just perfect for two. But if you want to feed a family of four, the recipe can easily be doubled in the same 10-inch skillet.

Prep Time:
15 Minutes

Start to Finish:
15 Minutes

**4 servings
(1½ cups each)**

Keep a couple jars of pesto on hand and you'll be able to elevate a handful of simple ingredients into a complex-tasting entrée. In this speedy dish, vegetables (fresh and frozen), chicken and pasta become much more than the sum of their parts with the addition of pesto and Gorgonzola.

Chicken Pesto Linguine

1   **package (9 oz) refrigerated linguine**

1   **cup red bell pepper strips**

1   **cup frozen sweet peas**

1   **container (7 oz) refrigerated basil pesto**

2   **packages (6 oz each) refrigerated grilled chicken breast strips**

1   **cup crumbled Gorgonzola cheese (4 oz)**

1   Fill 4-quart Dutch oven or saucepan two-thirds full of water; heat to boiling. Add linguine, bell pepper and peas; boil 2 to 3 minutes or until tender. Drain and return to Dutch oven.

2   Stir pesto, chicken and cheese into linguine mixture; cook over medium heat until thoroughly heated.

1 Serving: Calories 760; Total Fat 34g (Saturated Fat 11g, Trans Fat 0g); Cholesterol 95mg; Sodium 1290mg; Total Carbohydrate 70g (Dietary Fiber 6g); Protein 43g **Exchanges:** 4½ Starch, ½ Vegetable, 4 Very Lean Meat, 5½ Fat **Carbohydrate Choices:** 4½

> TRY THIS Leftover grilled chicken or cut-up deli rotisserie chicken can be substituted for the purchased grilled chicken breast strips; you'll need 2 cups.

> IF YOUR FAMILY isn't a fan of Gorgonzola, try feta cheese instead.

20 MINUTES OR LESS

Prep Time:
20 Minutes

Start to Finish:
20 Minutes

4 servings

Great citrus fruit is available any time of year, but it's seasonally at its peak in winter. Serve this bright-tasting dish in the coldest months for a reprieve from heavier winter dishes.

Fresh Citrus Chicken

> **GO-WITH IDEA** Pair this simple chicken dish with your favorite rice mix and steamed or roasted asparagus.

1	tablespoon vegetable oil	2	tablespoons fresh lime juice
4	boneless skinless chicken breasts (1 to 1¼ lb)	2	teaspoons chopped fresh cilantro
		⅛	teaspoon crushed red pepper flakes
3	cloves garlic, thinly sliced	1	medium orange, peeled, coarsely chopped
1	teaspoon grated lime peel		

1 In 12-inch skillet, heat oil over medium heat. Cook chicken and garlic in oil 8 to 10 minutes, turning chicken once and stirring garlic occasionally, until juice of chicken is clear when center of thickest part is cut (at least 165°F).

2 In small bowl, mix lime peel, lime juice, cilantro and pepper flakes. Pour into skillet. Place chopped orange on chicken. Cover; cook 1 to 2 minutes longer or until thoroughly heated. Serve any pan juices with chicken.

1 Serving: Calories 190; Total Fat 7g (Saturated Fat 1.5g, Trans Fat 0g); Cholesterol 70mg; Sodium 65mg; Total Carbohydrate 5g (Dietary Fiber 1g); Protein 26g **Exchanges:** ½ Starch, 3½ Very Lean Meat, 1 Fat **Carbohydrate Choices:** ½

Autumn is the perfect time to serve this dinner bursting with apple flavor. For a warm, satisfying meal, make mashed potatoes alongside and serve the chops and sauce over the potatoes.

25 MINUTES OR LESS

Prep Time:
25 Minutes

Start to Finish:
25 Minutes

4 servings

Pan-fried Pork Chops with Cider Sauce

4	boneless pork loin chops, ½ to ¾ inch thick (1 lb), trimmed of fat	⅛	teaspoon pepper
¼	teaspoon seasoned salt	1	tablespoon vegetable oil
¼	teaspoon dried thyme leaves	½	cup apple cider
⅛	teaspoon garlic powder	¼	cup brandy or apple cider
		1	tablespoon butter

1 Sprinkle both sides of pork chops with seasoned salt, thyme, garlic powder and pepper. In 12-inch skillet, heat oil over medium-high heat. Add pork; cook about 5 minutes or until bottoms are browned.

2 Turn pork chops; reduce heat to medium-low. Cook uncovered 5 to 10 minutes longer or until pork is no longer pink in center. Remove from skillet to plate; cover to keep warm.

3 Add cider and brandy to skillet. Heat to boiling, stirring to loosen browned bits from bottom of skillet; reduce heat to low. Add butter; simmer 1 to 3 minutes, stirring frequently, until slightly thickened. Serve sauce over pork.

1 Serving: Calories 250; Total Fat 15g (Saturated Fat 5g, Trans Fat 0g); Cholesterol 75mg; Sodium 150mg; Total Carbohydrate 4g (Dietary Fiber 0g); Protein 24g **Exchanges:** ½ Starch, 3 Lean Meat, 1 Fat **Carbohydrate Choices:** 0

> TRY THIS Bone-in pork loin chops, ½ inch thick, can be substituted for the boneless chops. Cook about 5 minutes on each side or until browned. Reduce heat to low. Cover; cook about 10 minutes longer or until pork is no longer pink in center.

> TRY THIS For pork chops with mustard cream sauce, omit cider, brandy and butter. Prepare recipe as directed through Step 2. Add ¼ cup dry sherry to skillet. Heat to boiling, stirring to loosen browned bits from bottom of skillet. Stir in ½ cup whipping cream, 1 tablespoon country-style Dijon mustard, 2 teaspoons chopped fresh chives, ⅛ teaspoon salt and ⅛ teaspoon pepper. Simmer 3 minutes, stirring frequently, until slightly thickened. Serve sauce over chops.

By keeping a well-stocked pantry, you'll always be ready to whip up a savory meal like this ravioli with bacon. Fresh spinach adds lift and brightness to the dish.

Prep Time:
20 Minutes

Start to Finish:
20 Minutes

4 servings
(1¼ cups each)

Bacon-Tomato-Spinach Ravioli Toss

2 packages (9 oz each) refrigerated cheese-filled ravioli	**3** cups fresh baby spinach leaves
6 slices packaged precooked bacon (from 2.1-oz package), broken into ½-inch pieces	**1** cup grape tomatoes, cut in half
	½ cup balsamic vinaigrette dressing
	¼ teaspoon freshly ground pepper

1 In 5-quart Dutch oven or stockpot, cook ravioli as directed on package; drain and return to Dutch oven. Meanwhile, on microwavable plate, microwave bacon 30 to 45 seconds on High until crisp.

2 Add bacon, spinach, tomatoes and dressing to ravioli. Cook over medium heat until warmed and spinach is partially wilted. Sprinkle with pepper.

1 Serving: Calories 500; Total Fat 18g (Saturated Fat 10g, Trans Fat 0g); Cholesterol 80mg; Sodium 660mg; Total Carbohydrate 63g (Dietary Fiber 3g); Protein 22g **Exchanges:** 4 Starch, 1 Vegetable, 1 High-Fat Meat, 1½ Fat **Carbohydrate Choices:** 4

> TIME-SAVER Buy prewashed spinach to save preparation time.

> TRY THIS Quartered cherry tomatoes or chopped plum (Roma) tomatoes can be substituted for the grape tomatoes.

Cajun seasoning amps up the flavor of this pasta dish and saves cooking time with a pre-combined mix of complementary spices. You'll love the smoky depth of flavor from the smoked sausage and fire-roasted tomatoes.

Prep Time:
30 Minutes

Start to Finish:
30 Minutes

6 servings
(1½ cups each)

Cajun Pasta with Smoked Sausage

8 oz uncooked fettuccine	1 can (28 oz) fire-roasted crushed tomatoes, undrained
2 tablespoons vegetable oil	1 tablespoon Cajun seasoning
1 large onion, chopped (1 cup)	½ cup whipping cream
2 medium red or green bell peppers or 1 of each, thinly sliced	½ cup shredded Parmesan cheese (2 oz)
3 cloves garlic, finely chopped	Chopped fresh parsley, if desired
1 package (14 oz) smoked sausage, cut into ½-inch slices	

1 Cook and drain fettuccine as directed on package.

2 Meanwhile, in 12-inch nonstick skillet, heat oil over medium-high heat. Cook onion, bell peppers and garlic in oil 3 to 4 minutes, stirring frequently, until crisp-tender. Add sausage; cook 3 to 4 minutes, stirring frequently, until vegetables are tender.

3 Add tomatoes and Cajun seasoning. Stir in whipping cream. Cook uncovered 5 to 8 minutes, stirring occasionally, until mixture has thickened.

4 In large serving bowl, toss sausage mixture and cooked fettuccine. Sprinkle with cheese and parsley.

1 Serving: Calories 560; Total Fat 35g (Saturated Fat 14g, Trans Fat 1g); Cholesterol 100mg; Sodium 1890mg; Total Carbohydrate 43g (Dietary Fiber 4g); Protein 18g **Exchanges:** 1½ Starch, 1 Other Carbohydrate, 1 Vegetable, ½ Lean Meat, 1 High-Fat Meat, 5 Fat **Carbohydrate Choices:** 3

> TRY THIS After tossing the fettuccine and sausage mixture, transfer to a 13x9-inch pan. Cover and refrigerate until ready to bake. Heat in a 375°F oven 30 to 40 minutes or until thoroughly heated.

15 MINUTES OR LESS

Just five ingredients and 15 minutes to a hearty weeknight dinner!

Prep Time:
15 Minutes

Start to Finish:
15 Minutes

4 servings
(1½ cups each)

Salami-Pesto Fusilli

2	cups uncooked fusilli pasta (6 oz)
1	container (7 oz) refrigerated basil pesto
1½	cups quartered cherry tomatoes

5 oz hard salami, cut into ½-inch cubes (about 1 cup)

⅔ cup shredded Parmesan cheese

1 Cook and drain pasta as directed on package.

2 In large serving bowl, toss hot pasta with pesto, tomatoes and salami. Sprinkle with cheese.

1 Serving: Calories 730; Total Fat 43g (Saturated Fat 13g, Trans Fat 0.5g); Cholesterol 55mg; Sodium 1640mg; Total Carbohydrate 56g (Dietary Fiber 5g); Protein 29g **Exchanges:** 3½ Starch, 1 Vegetable, 1 Medium-Fat Meat, 1 High-Fat Meat, 5½ Fat **Carbohydrate Choices:** 4

> FRESH FACT Genoa and cotto are among the best-known Italian salamis. Genoa is made of pork and veal, seasoned with garlic, pepper and red wine. Cotto is made of pork and beef, seasoned with garlic and studded with peppercorns. Use your favorite salami in this recipe.

Rather than opt for takeout, make this quick and economical Asian-inspired dish bursting with vegetables.

Prep Time:
20 Minutes

Start to Finish:
20 Minutes

4 servings
(1¾ cups each)

Beef-Mushroom Teriyaki Noodles

5 **cups uncooked fine egg noodles (8 oz)**	2 **green onions, diagonally sliced, green tops reserved**
1 **tablespoon vegetable oil**	1 **lb boneless beef sirloin steak, cut into thin bite-size strips**
1 **package (8 oz) sliced fresh mushrooms (about 3 cups)**	½ **cup teriyaki marinade and sauce (from 10-oz bottle)***
1 **cup julienne carrots (from 10-oz bag)**	2 **teaspoons cornstarch**
1 **cup red bell pepper strips**	

1 Cook and drain noodles as directed on package.

2 Meanwhile, in 12-inch nonstick skillet, heat oil over medium-high heat. Cook mushrooms, carrots, bell pepper and white portion of onions in oil 5 minutes, stirring occasionally, until soft. Remove mixture from skillet to bowl; cover to keep warm.

3 In same skillet, cook beef 1 to 2 minutes or just until beef begins to brown; drain. In small bowl, mix teriyaki marinade and cornstarch until blended. Stir teriyaki mixture and mushroom mixture into skillet with beef. Heat to boiling over medium heat, stirring constantly, until sauce is thickened.

4 In large serving bowl, toss cooked noodles with beef mixture and reserved green onion tops.

*Teriyaki marinade and sauce has a thin consistency. For best results, do not substitute teriyaki baste and glaze in this recipe.

1 Serving: Calories 450; Total Fat 11g (Saturated Fat 2.5g, Trans Fat 0g); Cholesterol 120mg; Sodium 1290mg; Total Carbohydrate 46g (Dietary Fiber 3g); Protein 41g **Exchanges:** 1½ Starch, 1 Other Carbohydrate, 1½ Vegetable, 2 Very Lean Meat, 3 Lean Meat **Carbohydrate Choices:** 3

> TRY THIS Freezing the meat for 30 to 60 minutes makes slicing it easier.

Chimichurri sauce is a versatile green sauce that originated in Argentina; you'll find many recipes to make this sauce, which beautifully complements grilled or cooked meat. Jarred pesto brings this sauce together quickly without necessitating the use of a blender or food processor.

Steak and Peppers in Chimichurri Sauce

½ **cup basil pesto**

1 **tablespoon lemon juice**

¼ **teaspoon dried oregano leaves**

⅛ **to ¼ teaspoon crushed red pepper flakes**

1 **tablespoon olive oil**

1 **medium onion, thinly sliced (about 1 cup)**

1 **medium orange bell pepper, cut into bite-size strips**

1 **medium yellow bell pepper, cut into bite-size strips**

1 **lb boneless beef sirloin steak, cut into 4 serving pieces**

1 **teaspoon garlic-pepper blend**

½ **teaspoon salt**

1 In medium heatproof bowl, mix pesto, lemon juice, oregano and pepper flakes; set aside.

2 In 12-inch nonstick skillet, heat oil over medium heat. Cook onion and bell peppers in oil 3 to 4 minutes, stirring frequently, until crisp-tender. Stir in pesto mixture. Return mixture to same bowl. Cover; set aside.

3 Sprinkle both sides of beef pieces with garlic-pepper blend and salt. Heat same skillet over medium-high heat. Add beef; cook 10 minutes, turning once.

4 Return vegetable mixture to skillet. Cook 1 to 2 minutes, stirring occasionally, until vegetables are hot and beef is of desired doneness (145°F for medium-rare). Serve pepper mixture over beef.

1 Serving: Calories 380; Total Fat 22g (Saturated Fat 4.5g, Trans Fat 0g); Cholesterol 85mg; Sodium 610mg; Total Carbohydrate 11g (Dietary Fiber 2g); Protein 34g **Exchanges:** ½ Starch, ½ Vegetable, 4½ Lean Meat, 1½ Fat **Carbohydrate Choices:** 1

While some recipes call for precooked shrimp, and this can be a time-saver, shrimp cooks so quickly that it's often preferable to purchase it raw and cook it yourself, controlling when it's ready.

Prep Time:
30 Minutes

Start to Finish:
30 Minutes

4 servings

Creole Shrimp Pasta

1¼ cups uncooked orzo pasta (8 oz)	3 cloves garlic, finely chopped
2 tablespoons olive oil	1 can (28 oz) diced tomatoes, undrained
1 large onion, chopped (1 cup)	2 teaspoons Cajun seasoning
2 stalks celery, thinly sliced (1 cup)	1 lb uncooked deveined peeled medium shrimp, thawed if frozen
2 small yellow or green bell peppers or 1 of each, chopped (1 cup)	Chopped fresh parsley, if desired

1 Cook and drain pasta as directed on package.

2 Meanwhile, in 12-inch nonstick skillet, heat oil over medium-high heat. Cook onion and celery in oil 3 to 5 minutes, stirring frequently, until vegetables begin to soften. Add bell peppers; cook 2 to 3 minutes. Add garlic; cook 30 seconds or until fragrant.

3 Stir in tomatoes and Cajun seasoning. Heat to boiling. Add shrimp. Cook and stir over medium-high heat until shrimp are pink and vegetables are crisp-tender.

4 To serve, spoon ¾ cup pasta into each of 4 shallow bowls; top each with 1½ cups shrimp mixture. Garnish with parsley.

1 Serving: Calories 460; Total Fat 9g (Saturated Fat 1.5g, Trans Fat 0g); Cholesterol 160mg; Sodium 1430mg; Total Carbohydrate 64g (Dietary Fiber 6g); Protein 29g **Exchanges:** 3½ Starch, ½ Other Carbohydrate, 1 Vegetable, 2½ Very Lean Meat, 1 Fat **Carbohydrate Choices:** 4

> TRY THIS If you don't have Cajun seasoning, substitute 1 to 1½ teaspoons dried thyme leaves and ½ teaspoon red pepper sauce.

> GO-WITH IDEA Serve this Louisiana favorite with warm biscuits, cold butter and a large bottle of red pepper sauce.

Gremolata is a condiment featuring chopped herbs, often including lemon. The gremolata mayonnaise in this recipe is simple to put together but greatly elevates the mild-tasting fish.

Prep Time:
15 Minutes

Start to Finish:
25 Minutes

4 servings

Seared Mackerel with Gremolata Mayonnaise

GREMOLATA MAYONNAISE

½   **cup mayonnaise**

2   **tablespoons chopped fresh parsley**

1   **teaspoon grated orange peel**

1   **teaspoon grated lemon peel**

TOASTED SPICE RUB

1   **tablespoon coriander seed**

2   **teaspoons cumin seed**

1   **teaspoon fennel seed**

1   **tablespoon sugar**

1   **teaspoon salt**

¼   **teaspoon pepper**

FISH

1¼   **lb mackerel, snapper, tilapia or other medium-firm fish fillets (about ½ inch thick)**

2   **tablespoons vegetable oil**

1 In small bowl, mix gremolata mayonnaise ingredients until well blended. Refrigerate until serving time.

2 Heat 8-inch skillet over medium-high heat. Add coriander, cumin and fennel seed; toast 2 to 3 minutes, stirring constantly, until coriander seed turns golden brown and mixture becomes fragrant. Place toasted spices in spice grinder. Grind until mixture looks like finely ground pepper. Transfer to small bowl; stir in sugar, salt and pepper.

3 Heat oven to 400°F. Rub tops of fish fillets with spice mixture; let stand 5 minutes. In 12-inch ovenproof skillet, heat oil over medium-high heat. Place fish, skin side down, in skillet; sear 2 minutes or until deep golden brown. Remove from heat. Carefully turn fish fillets over.

4 Bake 2 to 4 minutes or until fish flakes easily with fork. Serve with gremolata mayonnaise.

1 Serving: Calories 560; Total Fat 48g (Saturated Fat 9g, Trans Fat 0g); Cholesterol 95mg; Sodium 860mg; Total Carbohydrate 5g (Dietary Fiber 0g); Protein 27g **Exchanges:** ½ Other Carbohydrate, 4 Lean Meat, 7 Fat **Carbohydrate Choices:** ½

> GO WITH IDEA Serve this spiced mackerel with hot, cooked rice or couscous.

Prep Time:
10 Minutes

Start to Finish:
20 Minutes

4 servings

Your sheet-pan can do so much more than make cookies, as proven by this 20-minute protein- and flavor-packed shrimp dinner.

Spicy Shrimp Sheet-Pan Dinner

¼ **cup olive oil**	2 **cups halved cherry tomatoes**
2 **tablespoons chili garlic sauce**	1 **can (19 oz) chickpeas, drained, rinsed**
1 **tablespoon honey**	4 **cups baby spinach**
½ **teaspoon salt**	2 **oz crumbled feta cheese**
1 **lb uncooked deveined peeled large shrimp, tail shells removed**	

1 Position oven rack 4 inches from broiler. Set oven control to broil. Spray large, rimmed sheet-pan with cooking spray.

2 In large bowl, mix olive oil, chili garlic sauce, honey and salt. Add shrimp, tomatoes and chickpeas. Toss to coat, then pour in even layer on pan. Broil 5 minutes; stir, then broil 2 to 3 minutes longer or until shrimp are pink and cooked through.

3 Divide spinach among four plates. Top with shrimp mixture. Sprinkle with feta.

1 Serving: Calories 420 (Calories from Fat 180); Total Fat 20g (Saturated Fat 4.5g, Trans Fat 0g); Sodium 800mg; Total Carbohydrate 30g (Dietary Fiber 7g); Protein 30g **Exchanges:** 1½ Starch, 2 Vegetable, 3 Very Lean Meat, 3½ Fat **Carbohydrate Choices:** 2

> TRY THIS Like it spicy? Use up to 1 tablespoon more chili garlic sauce. Not a fan of feta? Try goat cheese, Parmesan or fresh mozzarella in its place.

Artichokes are often relegated to hot dips, but they are a wonderful vegetable to keep on hand. The combination of artichokes, tomatoes and fresh spinach works beautifully with the bay scallops. Serve this flavorful dish over hot, cooked angel hair pasta or linguine.

Scallops with Artichokes and Tomatoes

1 **lb bay scallops**	1 **box (9 oz) frozen artichoke hearts, thawed, drained***
4 **medium green onions, sliced (¼ cup)**	1 **cup cherry tomatoes, cut into quarters**
¼ **teaspoon salt**	1 **cup shredded fresh spinach leaves**
⅛ **teaspoon white pepper**	1 **tablespoon lemon juice**
1 **clove garlic, finely chopped**	

1 In 10-inch nonstick skillet, cook scallops, onions, salt, pepper and garlic over medium-high heat 4 minutes, stirring frequently, until scallops are white and opaque.

2 Stir in artichokes, tomatoes and spinach. Cook, stirring occasionally, until tomatoes are hot and spinach is wilted; drain. Sprinkle with lemon juice.

*A 14-ounce can of artichoke hearts, drained and cut into quarters, can be substituted for the frozen artichoke hearts.

1 Serving: Calories 110; Total Fat 1g (Saturated Fat 0g, Trans Fat 0g); Cholesterol 25mg; Sodium 580mg; Total Carbohydrate 12g (Dietary Fiber 5g); Protein 14g **Exchanges:** 2½ Vegetable, 1 Very Lean Meat **Carbohydrate Choices:** 1

Craving seafood tonight? Scallops, shrimp, and calamari come together in a light vegetable-packed skillet meal. This dish is delicious spooned over hot, cooked rice.

Citrus Seafood Skillet

1 tablespoon olive oil	½ lb uncooked deveined peeled medium shrimp, thawed if frozen
1 orange bell pepper, cut into ¼-inch strips	½ lb uncooked squid (calamari) tubes, thawed if frozen
½ medium red onion (halved lengthwise), sliced	½ teaspoon salt
1 tablespoon finely chopped seeded jalapeño chile	3 tablespoons fresh lime juice
½ lb bay scallops	2 teaspoons grated lime peel
	2 tablespoons chopped fresh cilantro

1 In 12-inch skillet, heat oil over medium-high heat. Cook bell pepper, onion and chile in oil 2 to 3 minutes, stirring occasionally, until crisp-tender.

2 Pat seafood dry with paper towels. Add scallops and shrimp to skillet; sprinkle seafood and vegetables with salt. Cook 3 to 4 minutes, adding calamari during last 1 minute of cooking, or until shrimp turn pink and scallops and calamari turn white and opaque. Add lime juice and lime peel; cook and stir just until thoroughly heated. Sprinkle with cilantro.

1 Serving: Calories 170; Total Fat 4.5g (Saturated Fat 1g, Trans Fat 0g); Cholesterol 210mg; Sodium 550mg; Total Carbohydrate 7g (Dietary Fiber 1g); Protein 24g **Exchanges:** ½ Other Carbohydrate, 3½ Very Lean Meat, ½ Fat **Carbohydrate Choices:** ½

> FRESH FACT If you love the flavors of ceviche, you'll find them all here in this quickly cooked dinner.

30 MINUTES OR LESS

Prep Time:
30 Minutes

Start to Finish:
30 Minutes

4 servings

Branzino is becoming very popular and is available at most markets. This mild fish makes a versatile meal, especially when paired with a unique sweet pea–mint pesto.

Branzino with Sweet Pea–Mint Pesto

TROUT

- 4 **pan-dressed branzino (about 8 oz each), heads removed if desired**
- 1 **tablespoon butter, melted**
- 1 **tablespoon lemon juice**
- ½ **teaspoon coarse sea salt**
- 4 **slices fresh lemon, cut in half**

SWEET PEA–MINT PESTO

- 1 **cup frozen sweet peas**
- ¼ **cup freshly grated Parmesan cheese**
- 3 **tablespoons olive oil**
- 2 **tablespoons finely chopped fresh mint leaves**
- 1 **tablespoon water**
- 1 **clove garlic**
- ¼ **teaspoon coarse sea salt**
- ¼ **teaspoon freshly ground pepper**

1 Heat oven to 400°F. Line 15x10x1-inch pan with foil. Rinse fish and pat dry with paper towel. Arrange fish in pan.

2 In small bowl, mix melted butter and lemon juice; brush mixture lightly on inside and outside of fish. Sprinkle inside of fish with salt; place 2 lemon half slices inside each. Bake 15 to 20 minutes or until fish flakes easily with fork.

3 Meanwhile, cook peas as directed on package. Rinse with cold water; drain well. In food processor, place peas and remaining pesto ingredients. Cover; process until smooth, stopping to scrape down side if necessary. Spoon pesto into serving bowl.

4 To serve, gently open fish if desired and, starting at head, loosen backbone and remove in one piece. Serve trout with pesto. Garnish with additional lemon slices and fresh mint, if desired.

1 Serving: Calories 460; Total Fat 28g (Saturated Fat 7g, Trans Fat 0g); Cholesterol 130mg; Sodium 700mg; Total Carbohydrate 6g (Dietary Fiber 1g); Protein 45g **Exchanges:** ½ Starch, 6 Very Lean Meat, 5 Fat **Carbohydrate Choices:** ½

> **FRESH FACT** The term "pan-dressed" refers to a whole fish that has been split open and its internal organs removed. If the fish has hard or rough scales, those are often removed, too. The head, tail and fins are usually left on small fish such as trout. You can ask the seafood department to remove those for you, or they can be easily cut off with a chef's knife at home.

Stovetop and Roasted Foods **143**

Salmon is endlessly versatile and works particularly well with this citrus and garlic glaze. For a complete meal, serve over hot, cooked orzo pasta with some sautéed greens on the side.

Prep Time:
10 Minutes

Start to Finish:
30 Minutes

4 servings

Citrus-Glazed Salmon

1	salmon fillet (1¼ lb), cut into 4 serving pieces	½	teaspoon salt
2	medium limes	4	cloves garlic, finely chopped
1	small orange	2	medium green onions, sliced (2 tablespoons)
⅓	cup agave syrup	1	lime slice, cut into 4 wedges
1	teaspoon pepper	1	orange slice, cut into 4 wedges

1 Heat oven to 400°F. Line 15x10x1-inch pan with cooking parchment paper or foil. Place salmon, skin side down, in pan.

2 Grate lime peel into small bowl. Squeeze enough juice to equal 2 tablespoons; add to bowl. Grate orange peel into bowl. Squeeze enough juice to equal 2 tablespoons; add to peel mixture. Stir in agave syrup, pepper, salt and garlic. Remove ¼ cup citrus mixture; set remaining citrus mixture aside. Brush tops and sides of salmon with ¼ cup citrus mixture.

3 Bake 13 to 17 minutes or until fish flakes easily with fork. With metal spatula, lift each salmon piece from skin and place on plate. Sprinkle with onions; top with lime and orange wedges. Drizzle with reserved citrus mixture.

1 Serving: Calories 320; Total Fat 9g (Saturated Fat 1.5g, Trans Fat 0g); Cholesterol 80mg; Sodium 360mg; Total Carbohydrate 30g (Dietary Fiber 3g); Protein 29g **Exchanges:** ½ Fruit, 1½ Other Carbohydrate, 2 Very Lean Meat, 2 Lean Meat, ½ Fat **Carbohydrate Choices:** 2

Prep Time:
30 Minutes

Start to Finish:
30 Minutes

4 servings

Fish and salsa are a wonderful combination, but don't restrict your fish toppings. Canned beans mixed with grilled tomato and fragrant rosemary are an aromatic and delicious combination with mild-flavored varieties such as flounder or cod.

Fish with Tomato and Cannellini Relish

1 lb mild-flavored, medium to medium-firm fish fillets (catfish, flounder or cod), cut into 4 serving pieces	4 teaspoons olive oil
½ teaspoon salt	1 can (19 oz) cannellini beans, drained, rinsed
⅛ teaspoon pepper	1 clove garlic, finely chopped
3 tablespoons fresh lemon juice	1 teaspoon chopped fresh rosemary leaves or ¼ teaspoon dried rosemary leaves, crushed
4 medium plum (Roma) tomatoes, cut lengthwise in half	Lemon wedges
	Fresh rosemary sprigs, if desired

1 Sprinkle fish with ¼ teaspoon of the salt and the pepper; drizzle with 1 tablespoon of the lemon juice. Set aside.

2 Heat nonstick or well-seasoned grill pan or skillet over medium heat. Brush tomatoes with 1 teaspoon of the oil. Add tomato halves, cut sides down, to grill pan. Cook 6 to 8 minutes, turning once, until very tender. Remove tomatoes from pan; cool slightly.

3 Place fish fillets on grill pan. Cook 4 to 6 minutes per ½-inch thickness, turning once, until fish flakes easily with fork.

4 Coarsely chop grilled tomatoes. In medium bowl, gently toss tomatoes, beans, garlic, chopped rosemary and remaining 2 tablespoons lemon juice, 3 teaspoons oil and ¼ teaspoon salt.

5 To serve, place ½ cup tomato-bean relish on each of 4 plates. Place fish on relish. Serve with lemon; garnish with rosemary sprigs.

1 Serving: Calories 350; Total Fat 7g (Saturated Fat 1g, Trans Fat 0g); Cholesterol 60mg; Sodium 400mg; Total Carbohydrate 38g (Dietary Fiber 9g); Protein 35g **Exchanges:** 2 Starch, 1 Vegetable, 2 Very Lean Meat, 2 Lean Meat **Carbohydrate Choices:** 2½

This simple and quick-to-prepare salad makes an elegant luncheon or easy dinner. Boil a dozen eggs at a time and keep them in the fridge for healthy snacking and as ingredients in dishes such as this one.

Prep Time:
15 Minutes

Start to Finish:
15 Minutes

4 servings

Easy Noodles Niçoise

2	cups fresh green beans, cut into 1-inch pieces (about 8 oz)
8	oz uncooked vermicelli
¾	cup Caesar dressing
1	can (12 oz) white albacore tuna, drained
12	pitted kalamata or ripe olives
4	hard-cooked eggs, sliced
¼	cup sliced radishes

1 Fill 5-quart Dutch oven or stockpot two-thirds full of water; heat to boiling. Add beans; boil 1 minute. Add vermicelli; boil 6 minutes. Drain. Rinse with cold water to cool; drain and return to Dutch oven. Add ½ cup of the dressing; toss to coat.

2 Divide vermicelli mixture among 4 plates. Mound one-fourth of the tuna in center of each plate; surround with olives, eggs and radishes. Drizzle remaining ¼ cup dressing evenly over salads.

1 Serving: Calories 670; Total Fat 34g (Saturated Fat 6g, Trans Fat 0g); Cholesterol 250mg; Sodium 1090mg; Total Carbohydrate 56g (Dietary Fiber 5g); Protein 34g **Exchanges:** 3½ Starch, 1 Vegetable, 3 Lean Meat, 4½ Fat **Carbohydrate Choices:** 4

> **TIME-SAVER** Hard-cooked eggs can be purchased in the deli or dairy section of the grocery store.

30 MINUTES OR LESS

Risotto has a reputation for being time-consuming or difficult to make. In fact, it is a lovely and simple-to-make supper. Purchasing ready-to-use butternut squash makes this sophisticated meal extra-convenient.

Prep Time:
30 Minutes

Start to Finish:
30 Minutes

4 servings
(1¼ cups each)

Butternut Squash Risotto

1   carton (32 oz) vegetable broth (4 cups)

1   tablespoon olive oil

1   medium onion, chopped (½ cup)

2   cups ready-to-use cubed fresh butternut squash (from 16-oz package)

¼   cup dry white wine or vegetable broth

1   cup uncooked short-grain Arborio rice or regular long-grain white rice

1   tablespoon garlic-and-herb seasoning

1   cup grated Parmesan cheese

1   bag (6 oz) fresh baby spinach leaves

1 In 1½-quart saucepan, heat broth over medium-high heat just until simmering. Keep broth at a simmer.

2 In 5-quart Dutch oven, heat oil over medium-high heat. Cook onion and squash in oil 3 minutes, stirring occasionally, just until onion starts to soften. Add wine; cook until liquid is almost completely evaporated. Stir in rice and 1 teaspoon of the garlic-and-herb seasoning. Cook 2 minutes, stirring frequently, until light brown.

3 Stir in 1 cup of the hot broth. Cook uncovered about 3 minutes, stirring frequently, until broth is absorbed; repeat with 2 more cups broth, adding 1 cup at a time. Stir in remaining 1 cup broth. Cook about 3 minutes longer, stirring frequently, until rice is just tender and mixture is creamy.

4 Add remaining 2 teaspoons garlic-and-herb seasoning, the cheese and spinach. Cook and stir just until spinach wilts. Serve immediately.

1 Serving: Calories 380; Total Fat 11g (Saturated Fat 5g, Trans Fat 0g); Cholesterol 20mg; Sodium 1740mg; Total Carbohydrate 54g (Dietary Fiber 2g); Protein 15g **Exchanges:** 3 Starch, 2 Vegetable, ½ Lean Meat, 1½ Fat **Carbohydrate Choices:** 3½

> FRESH FACT Many grocery and warehouse stores sell packages of ready-to-use, cut-up butternut squash, which really saves on prep time. If this product is not available, a 1¼-pound butternut squash, peeled, seeded and cubed, will yield about 2 cups.

30 MINUTES OR LESS

Prep Time:
30 Minutes

Start to Finish:
30 Minutes

**4 servings
(1¼ cups each)**

Broccoli rabe adds a fresh and unexpected complement to orecchiette pasta. Your family will love the rich brown butter sauce and the delicious crunch of pine nuts.

Browned Butter Orecchiette with Broccoli Rabe

1 lb broccoli rabe (rapini)	1 package (8.8 oz) orecchiette (tiny disk) pasta (about 6¾ cups uncooked)
⅓ cup butter	**Toasted pine nuts or chopped walnuts, if desired**
1 tablespoon fresh lemon juice	**Shredded Parmesan cheese, if desired**
½ teaspoon salt	

1 Cut off tough stem ends (about 1 inch) from broccoli rabe and discard. Cut remaining stems into 1-inch pieces. Cut leaves crosswise into 2-inch pieces (about 10 loosely packed cups). Cut any florets into bite-size pieces if necessary. Set aside.

2 In 1-quart saucepan, heat butter over medium heat, stirring constantly, until medium golden brown. (Watch carefully because butter can brown and then burn quickly.) Remove from heat; stir in lemon juice and salt.

3 Cook and drain pasta as directed on package—except add reserved broccoli rabe stems during last 5 minutes of cooking.

4 Meanwhile, in 12-inch nonstick skillet, heat 1 tablespoon of the browned butter over medium heat. Add reserved broccoli rabe leaves and florets; cook 4 to 6 minutes, stirring frequently, until leaves are wilted. Add pasta mixture and remaining browned butter; toss to coat. Heat until hot. Sprinkle with nuts and cheese.

1 Serving: Calories 450; Total Fat 17g (Saturated Fat 10g, Trans Fat 0.5g); Cholesterol 40mg; Sodium 710mg; Total Carbohydrate 61g (Dietary Fiber 6g); Protein 13g **Exchanges:** 3½ Starch, 1 Vegetable, 3 Fat **Carbohydrate Choices:** 4

Broccoli Rabe

Also known as rapini, broccoli rabe (or raab) is part of both the cabbage and turnip family of vegetables. It has 6- to 9-inch stalks and scattered clusters of broccoli-like buds. This Italian favorite has a distinctive nutty but slightly bitter flavor and can be cooked many ways.

Purchase broccoli rabe that is crisp and green and fresh-looking. Store it in the refrigerator, loosely wrapped in a plastic bag, for up to three days. To cook broccoli rabe, wash thoroughly and remove the tough ends of the stems—about an inch.

Try one of the following ideas using broccoli rabe.

PESTO CHICKEN AND BROCCOLI RABE PIZZA Spread a purchased pizza crust with ¼ cup refrigerated or homemade pesto, ¾ cup shredded cooked chicken, 1½ cups sliced broccoli rabe and 1 cup shredded mozzarella cheese. Bake pizza as directed on pizza crust package.

BROCCOLI RABE WITH GARLIC AND BACON In 10-inch skillet, cook 2 slices cut-up bacon over medium heat 3 to 5 minutes or until crisp. Stir in 2 cups cut-up broccoli rabe and 1 finely chopped garlic clove. Cook and stir 4 to 6 minutes or until broccoli rabe is fork-tender.

CANADIAN BACON AND BROCCOLI RABE SANDWICHES For each sandwich, spread 2 slices whole-grain bread with 1 tablespoon mustard-mayonnaise. Place about ½ cup sliced broccoli rabe on 1 slice; top with 2 to 3 slices Canadian bacon and 1 slice mozzarella cheese. Top with remaining bread slice, mustard mixture side down. Spread outsides of sandwich with butter. Cook in skillet over medium-low heat 3 to 4 minutes on each side or until toasted and cheese is melted.

MEATBALLS AND BROCCOLI RABE In 10-inch skillet heat 1 tablespoon olive oil. Cook 2 cups sliced broccoli rabe in oil 3 to 4 minutes or until fork-tender. Stir in 8 ounces thawed, cooked Italian meatballs and ¼ cup roasted red pepper. Cook and stir until thoroughly heated; stir in 2 tablespoons chopped fresh basil.

BROCCOLI RABE WITH PASTA In 10-inch skillet, heat 1 can diced tomatoes with oregano, garlic and basil over medium heat until hot. Stir in 2 to 3 cups cut-up broccoli rabe. Serve over hot orecchiette pasta; sprinkle with shredded fresh Parmesan cheese.

BROCCOLI RABE WITH CARROTS In 10-inch skillet, cook 1 cup julienne-cut carrots and ½ cup sliced onion in 1 tablespoon olive oil 3 to 4 minutes or until fork-tender. Stir in 2 cups cut-up broccoli rabe and 1 tablespoon chopped fresh oregano. Cook 3 to 4 minutes or until broccoli rabe is just tender.

Kids love this delicious cheese-laced spaghetti dish, and adults love the elegance that is lent by Pecorino Romano cheese and the richness of olive oil.

Prep Time:
25 Minutes

Start to Finish:
25 Minutes

6 servings
(1 cup each)

Cacio e Pepe

5 quarts water	2 teaspoons coarse ground black pepper
1 tablespoon salt	1½ cups finely shredded Pecorino Romano cheese (6 oz)
1 package (16 oz) spaghetti	Chopped fresh parsley, if desired
¼ cup olive oil	

1 In 8-quart Dutch oven or stockpot, heat water and salt to boiling. Add spaghetti; cook as directed on package. Remove 1 cup of the cooking water; set aside. Drain spaghetti but do not rinse; set aside.

2 In Dutch oven, heat oil over medium heat. Add pepper; cook 1 minute, stirring constantly. Add ¾ cup of the cooking water; heat until simmering. Add spaghetti; sprinkle with cheese. Toss with tongs until mixture clings to spaghetti. If mixture seems dry, add remaining ¼ cup reserved cooking water (pasta dish will not be saucy).

3 Sprinkle with parsley. Serve with additional cheese, if desired.

1 Serving: Calories 520; Total Fat 19g (Saturated Fat 6g, Trans Fat 0g); Cholesterol 30mg; Sodium 640mg; Total Carbohydrate 67g (Dietary Fiber 4g); Protein 21g **Exchanges:** 4 Starch, ½ Other Carbohydrate, 1 High-Fat Meat, 2 Fat **Carbohydrate Choices:** 4½

> FRESH FACT Cacio e Pepe translates to "cheese and pepper"—and the recipe really does have 2 teaspoons of pepper. For those a bit faint of heart, go ahead and use half that amount.

Prep Time:
15 Minutes

Start to Finish:
15 Minutes

6 servings

This super-fast dish comes together with creamy avocado. When choosing avocados, look for those that are firm but just slightly soft when lightly pressed. There should be no soft spots or signs of decay. If avocados are not quite ripe, store them at room temperature for a day or two.

Angel Hair Pasta with Basil, Avocado and Tomatoes

8 oz uncooked angel hair (capellini) pasta	1 ripe small avocado, pitted, peeled and diced
2 tablespoons olive or vegetable oil	4 medium tomatoes, cut into small cubes
2 cloves garlic, finely chopped	½ teaspoon salt
¾ cup chopped fresh basil leaves	¼ teaspoon pepper

1 Cook and drain pasta as directed on package.

2 Meanwhile, in 3-quart saucepan, heat oil over medium heat. Cook garlic in oil about 5 minutes, stirring occasionally, until tender but not brown. Remove from heat; stir in basil, avocado and tomatoes.

3 In large serving bowl, gently toss vegetable mixture with cooked pasta. Sprinkle with salt and pepper.

1 Serving: Calories 260; Total Fat 8g (Saturated Fat 1g, Trans Fat 0g); Cholesterol 0mg; Sodium 350mg; Total Carbohydrate 38g (Dietary Fiber 4g); Protein 7g **Exchanges:** 2 Starch, 1 Vegetable, 1½ Fat **Carbohydrate Choices:** 2½

> TRY THIS Add 1 cup shredded cooked chicken, or ½ pound cooked medium shrimp, with the tomatoes. Cook and stir just until heated.

Prep Time:
30 Minutes

Start to Finish:
30 Minutes

6 servings

Portabella mushrooms have a meatier feel than white button mushrooms. You can also try cremini mushrooms in this recipe, which are just young portabellas; they are about the size of white button mushrooms but have more depth of flavor.

Penne with Portabella Mushrooms and Fennel

2½ **cups uncooked penne pasta (about 8 oz)**	1 **jar (1 lb 8 oz) chunky tomato pasta sauce (any meatless variety)**
2 **tablespoons olive oil**	1 **can (15 oz) cannellini beans, drained**
1 **package (8 oz) fresh portabella mushrooms, sliced**	3 **tablespoons chopped fresh or 1 tablespoon dried basil leaves**
1 **bulb fennel, trimmed, cut into 1-inch slices**	½ **cup shredded Asiago or Parmesan cheese (2 oz)**
2 **cloves garlic, finely chopped**	**Fennel leaves, if desired**

1 Cook and drain pasta as directed on package.

2 Meanwhile, in 10-inch skillet, heat oil over medium heat. Cook mushrooms, fennel and garlic in oil 5 to 6 minutes, stirring occasionally, until fennel is crisp-tender. Stir in pasta sauce, beans and basil. Cook, stirring occasionally, until thoroughly heated.

3 Divide cooked pasta among 6 bowls or plates; spoon vegetable mixture evenly over pasta. Sprinkle with cheese. Garnish with fennel leaves.

1 Serving: Calories 490; Total Fat 15g (Saturated Fat 4g, Trans Fat 0g); Cholesterol 10mg; Sodium 900mg; Total Carbohydrate 73g (Dietary Fiber 8g); Protein 16g **Exchanges:** 2 Starch, 2 Other Carbohydrate, 2½ Vegetable, 1 Very Lean Meat, 2½ Fat **Carbohydrate Choices:** 5

> TRY THIS You can use any beans you like in this recipe. Try great northern beans, garbanzo beans or kidney beans.

> GO-WITH IDEA Serve with crusty French bread or whole-grain dinner rolls and a spinach salad with raspberry vinaigrette.

Pesto is often associated solely with basil, but practically any greens can make pesto—including greens like chard, radish tops and kale. Parsley joins the basil for a two-herb combination that tops ravioli beautifully.

Prep Time:
25 Minutes

Start to Finish:
25 Minutes

6 servings
(1 cup each)

Italian Parsley–Pesto Ravioli

1   package (20 oz) refrigerated cheese-filled ravioli

2   cups fresh Italian (flat-leaf) parsley

1   cup fresh basil leaves

1   clove garlic, peeled

1   cup grated Parmesan cheese

¾   cup chopped walnuts

¼   cup olive oil

¼   cup reduced-sodium chicken broth

½   cup chopped drained roasted red bell peppers (from a jar)

1   Cook and drain ravioli as directed on package.

2   Meanwhile, in blender or food processor, place parsley, basil, garlic, ½ cup of the cheese, ¼ cup of the walnuts, the oil and broth. Cover; blend on medium speed about 3 minutes, stopping occasionally to scrape sides, until almost smooth.

3   In large serving bowl, toss pesto with cooked ravioli. Garnish with roasted peppers and remaining ½ cup walnuts. Serve with remaining ½ cup cheese.

1 Serving: Calories 580; Total Fat 34g (Saturated Fat 11g, Trans Fat 0g); Cholesterol 65mg; Sodium 720mg; Total Carbohydrate 46g (Dietary Fiber 3g); Protein 22g **Exchanges:** 2½ Starch, 1 Vegetable, 1 Lean Meat, 1 Medium-Fat Meat, 5 Fat **Carbohydrate Choices:** 3

Think of tofu as a blank slate; it has the delightful attribute of taking on the flavors with it. The Italian dressing that these tofu steaks marinate in imparts a zesty flavor that works perfectly with the fresh vegetables.

Prep Time:
15 Minutes

Start to Finish:
30 Minutes

6 servings

Breaded Tofu Steaks with Cucumber Salad

1 **package (18 oz) extra-firm tofu, drained, sliced into 6 steaks, ½ inch thick**	1 **small cucumber, seeded, chopped (1 cup)**
¾ **cup Italian dressing**	2 **green onions, thinly sliced (2 tablespoons)**
½ **cup drained whole kernel sweet corn (from 11-oz can)**	2 **cups four-cheese Italian-herb baked cheese crispy crackers (from 5.9-oz box), crushed**
1 **red bell pepper, chopped (1 cup)**	

1 Heat oven to 425°F. On cookie sheet, place tofu between several layers of paper towels. Place second cookie sheet, with about 5 lb weight, on top of paper towels. (Use 15- or 16-oz cans from pantry for weight.) Let tofu drain 5 minutes.

2 In 1-gallon resealable plastic food-storage bag, place tofu; pour ½ cup dressing over tofu in bag. Seal bag; gently rotate to coat. Let stand 5 minutes to marinate.

3 Meanwhile, in medium bowl, stir together corn, bell pepper, cucumber and onions. Add remaining ¼ cup dressing; toss to coat. Set aside.

4 Place cracker crumbs in shallow dish. Remove tofu from marinade; discard marinade. Coat tofu in crumbs, pressing in lightly on both sides. Place on cookie sheet.

5 Bake 12 to 15 minutes or until golden brown. To serve, top each tofu steak with about ⅓ cup bell pepper-cucumber salad.

1 Serving: Calories 240; Total Fat 15g (Saturated Fat 1g, Trans Fat 0g); Cholesterol 0mg; Sodium 680mg; Total Carbohydrate 18g (Dietary Fiber 2g); Protein 8g **Exchanges:** ½ Starch, ½ Other Carbohydrate, ½ Vegetable, 1 Very Lean Meat, 3 Fat **Carbohydrate Choices:** 1

> FRESH FACT Tofu comes in several firmness levels. Extra-firm tofu is key for getting the "steak" consistency that is desired for this dish.

CHAPTER 4

Grilled and Broiled Choices

Bacon, poblano chiles and smoky spices come together for an exotic meal that is destined to become a family favorite!

Prep Time:
30 Minutes

Start to Finish:
30 Minutes

4 servings

Bacon-Wrapped Chicken and Chiles

SPICE RUB

- 2½ teaspoons chili powder
- 1½ teaspoons ground cumin
- 1 teaspoon salt
- 1 teaspoon garlic powder

CHICKEN AND VEGETABLES

- 4 boneless skinless chicken breasts (1¼ lb)
- 4 slices bacon
- 2 medium poblano chiles
- 3 medium sweet potatoes (1½ lb), peeled, each cut lengthwise into 8 wedges
- 3 tablespoons vegetable oil

1 Spray grill rack with cooking spray. Spray 16x12-inch perforated grill pan with cooking spray. Heat gas or charcoal grill. In small bowl, mix spice rub ingredients.

2 Sprinkle both sides of chicken with 1 tablespoon of the spice rub; press and rub into chicken. Wrap each chicken breast with 1 slice bacon, stretching bacon gently to cover as much of the chicken as possible; secure ends of bacon with toothpicks.

3 Cut each chile lengthwise in half; remove seeds and stems. Cut chiles into quarters. In 2-gallon resealable food-storage plastic bag, place chiles, sweet potatoes, oil and remaining spice rub. Seal bag; shake to coat.

4 Arrange potatoes and chiles in single layer on grill pan; place pan on one side of grill. Place chicken on other side of grill. Cover grill; cook over medium heat 12 to 15 minutes, turning potatoes and chiles twice and turning chicken once, until potatoes are tender and juice of chicken is clear when center of thickest part is cut (at least 165°F).

1 Serving: Calories 430; Total Fat 19g (Saturated Fat 4g, Trans Fat 0g); Cholesterol 110mg; Sodium 900mg; Total Carbohydrate 22g (Dietary Fiber 4g); Protein 42g **Exchanges:** ½ Starch, ½ Other Carbohydrate, 1 Vegetable, 5½ Very Lean Meat, 3 Fat **Carbohydrate Choices:** 1½

> FRESH FACT Poblano chiles are triangle- or heart-shaped, about 2½ to 3 inches across at the widest part and 4 to 5 inches long. They are dark green in color—sometimes almost black—and range from mild to hot in flavor. If you can't find them, use milder Anaheim chiles.

Quick-cooking kabobs—like these teriyaki-glazed chicken skewers—are a great dinner choice when time is tight.

Prep Time:
25 Minutes

Start to Finish:
25 Minutes

4 servings

Asian Chicken Kabobs

1   lb boneless skinless chicken breasts, cut into 24 (1-inch) cubes

1   red bell pepper, cut into 8 (1-inch) pieces

½   red onion, cut into 8 wedges, separated into layers

8   medium mushrooms

½   cup teriyaki baste and glaze (from 12-oz bottle)

Chopped fresh cilantro, if desired

Lime wedges, if desired

1   Heat gas or charcoal grill. On 4 (12-inch) skewers, alternately thread chicken and vegetables, leaving about ¼-inch space between each piece.*

2   Place skewers on grill over medium heat. Cover grill; cook 10 to 11 minutes, turning occasionally, until chicken is no longer pink in center and vegetables are done as desired. During last 2 to 3 minutes of cooking, brush kabobs generously with teriyaki glaze and turn frequently. Sprinkle with cilantro; serve with lime wedges.

*If using bamboo skewers, soak in water at least 30 minutes before using to prevent burning.

1 Serving: Calories 180; Total Fat 3.5g (Saturated Fat 1g, Trans Fat 0g); Cholesterol 65mg; Sodium 1440mg; Total Carbohydrate 10g (Dietary Fiber 1g); Protein 27g **Exchanges:** 1½ Vegetable, 3½ Very Lean Meat, ½ Fat **Carbohydrate Choices:** ½

> TRY THIS Substitute your favorite vegetables in these kabobs. For example, use 1 small zucchini, sliced about ¾ inch thick, instead of the onion.

Prep Time:
30 Minutes

Start to Finish:
30 Minutes

4 servings

Fun and tasty! A rosemary-lemon marinade gives these grilled kabobs loads of flavor.

Mediterranean Chicken-Vegetable Kabobs

ROSEMARY-LEMON BASTING SAUCE

¼ **cup lemon juice**

3 **tablespoons olive or vegetable oil**

2 **teaspoons chopped fresh rosemary leaves**

½ **teaspoon salt**

¼ **teaspoon pepper**

4 **cloves garlic, finely chopped**

CHICKEN AND VEGETABLES

1 **lb boneless skinless chicken breasts, cut into 1½-inch pieces**

1 **medium red bell pepper, cut into 1-inch pieces**

1 **medium zucchini, cut into 1-inch pieces**

1 **medium red onion, cut into wedges**

1 **lb fresh asparagus spears, trimmed**

¼ **cup crumbled feta cheese (1 oz)**

1 Heat gas or charcoal grill. In small bowl, mix basting sauce ingredients.

2 On 4 (15-inch) metal skewers, alternately thread chicken and vegetables, leaving about ¼-inch space between each piece. Brush with basting sauce.

3 Place kabobs on grill over medium heat. Cover grill; cook 10 to 15 minutes, turning and brushing frequently with sauce, until chicken is no longer pink in center. Add asparagus to grill for last 5 minutes of cooking, turning occasionally, until crisp-tender. Discard any remaining basting sauce. Sprinkle cheese over kabobs. Serve with asparagus.

1 Serving: Calories 320; Total Fat 16g (Saturated Fat 4g, Trans Fat 0g); Cholesterol 80mg; Sodium 470mg; Total Carbohydrate 13g (Dietary Fiber 4g); Protein 31g **Exchanges:** 3 Vegetable, 3½ Very Lean Meat, 3 Fat **Carbohydrate Choices:** 1

> TRY THIS If you have time, marinate the chicken before grilling. In shallow glass or plastic bowl, mix basting sauce ingredients; add chicken and stir to coat. Cover and refrigerate at least 30 minutes but no longer than 6 hours, stirring occasionally. After threading chicken, reserve marinade to brush on chicken and vegetables during grilling.

Prep Time:
30 Minutes

Start to Finish:
30 Minutes

4 servings

Grilled chicken breasts "go green" with mint, chives and sweet peas. Served atop linguine, it's a complete meal in 30 minutes.

Minty Linguine with Grilled Chicken

4	boneless skinless chicken breasts (1¼ lb)	¼	teaspoon pepper
½	cup olive oil	8	oz uncooked linguine
1	teaspoon garlic-pepper blend	1	box (9 oz) frozen baby sweet peas
⅔	cup lightly packed fresh mint leaves	1	cup small fresh mozzarella cheese balls (6 oz)
2	tablespoons lemon juice	¼	cup chopped fresh chives
½	teaspoon salt		

> FRESH FACT Fresh mozzarella is packed in liquid and is very mild and sweet tasting. Look for small, fresh, pearl-size mozzarella balls called Perline, but if unavailable, use any size fresh mozzarella and cut it into ½-inch pieces. Fresh mozzarella does not melt; instead it softens when heated. Regular mozzarella, cubed or shredded, can also be used in this recipe.

1 Heat gas or charcoal grill. Brush both sides of chicken with 1 tablespoon of the oil; sprinkle with garlic-pepper blend. In blender, place remaining oil, the mint, lemon juice, salt and pepper. Cover; blend until smooth. Set aside.

2 Place chicken on grill over medium heat. Cover grill; cook 10 to 12 minutes, turning once, until juice of chicken is clear when center of thickest part is cut (at least 165°F). Remove chicken from grill to cutting board. Loosely cover; let stand 3 minutes.

3 Meanwhile, cook and drain linguine as directed on package, adding peas during last 3 minutes of cooking. Toss linguine and peas with reserved mint mixture and the mozzarella; cover to keep warm.

4 Slice chicken crosswise. Place linguine mixture on platter or individual plates; arrange chicken on top. Sprinkle with chives.

1 Serving: Calories 850; Total Fat 44g (Saturated Fat 12g, Trans Fat 0g); Cholesterol 125mg; Sodium 930mg; Total Carbohydrate 60g (Dietary Fiber 6g); Protein 54g **Exchanges:** 3 Starch, ½ Other Carbohydrate, 1 Vegetable, 5 Very Lean Meat, 1 Medium-Fat Meat, 7 Fat **Carbohydrate Choices:** 4

Prep Time:
30 Minutes

Start to Finish:
30 Minutes

4 servings

Try chicken legs for a tasty change of pace. Grilled and glazed, these make a simple 30-minute main dish combining the sweetness of honey and tangy acidity of lemon. A tossed salad and some wild rice would make great accompaniments.

Lemon-Thyme Chicken Legs

¼	cup honey	½	teaspoon dried thyme leaves
1	tablespoon grated lemon peel	½	teaspoon pepper
1	tablespoon lemon juice	8	chicken legs (about 2½ lb)
1	teaspoon salt		Lemon wedges, if desired

1 Heat gas or charcoal grill. In small bowl, mix honey, lemon peel, lemon juice, ½ teaspoon of the salt, the thyme and ¼ teaspoon of the pepper; set aside.

2 Sprinkle chicken with remaining ½ teaspoon salt and ¼ teaspoon pepper. Place chicken on grill over medium heat. Cover grill; cook 16 to 20 minutes, turning once, until juice of chicken is clear when thickest part is cut to bone (at least 165°F).

3 Brush chicken generously with lemon-honey sauce, turning to coat evenly. Cover grill; cook 1 to 2 minutes longer on each side or until glaze is hot and bubbly. Garnish with lemon wedges.

1 Serving: Calories 590; Total Fat 31g (Saturated Fat 8g, Trans Fat 0.5g); Cholesterol 210mg; Sodium 790mg; Total Carbohydrate 18g (Dietary Fiber 0g); Protein 59g **Exchanges:** 1 Other Carbohydrate, 8½ Very Lean Meat, 5½ Fat **Carbohydrate Choices:** 1

> TRY THIS The lemon-honey sauce would also be great on other chicken pieces. Prepare as directed, adjusting the grilling time as needed; grill smaller pieces 10 to 15 minutes and larger pieces 20 to 40 minutes. Check doneness with a meat thermometer inserted into the center of the meat, not touching bone; when done, it should read at least 165°F. Be sure to grill the chicken until it is completely cooked before brushing with the sauce.

Can't decide between burgers and Mexican food? Combine 'em in this spicy turkey cheeseburger.

25 MINUTES OR LESS

Prep Time:
25 Minutes

Start to Finish:
25 Minutes

4 burgers

Turkey-Cheddar-Chipotle Burgers

1	package (20 oz) ground turkey	½	teaspoon salt
2	chipotle chiles in adobo sauce (from 7-oz can), finely chopped	4	slices Cheddar cheese
3	ounces Cheddar cheese, cut into ½-inch pieces (½ cup)	4	burger buns, split
		4	leaves leaf lettuce, if desired
		¼	cup salsa

1 Heat gas or charcoal grill. In large bowl, mix turkey, chiles, cheese pieces and salt. Shape mixture into 4 patties, about ¾ inch thick.

2 Place patties on grill over medium heat. Cover grill; cook 13 to 15 minutes, turning once, until meat thermometer inserted in center of patties reads 165°F. Top each burger with 1 slice cheese. Cover grill; cook about 30 seconds longer or until cheese begins to melt.

3 On bun bottoms, place lettuce and burgers; top each with 1 tablespoon salsa. Cover with bun tops.

1 Burger: Calories 450; Total Fat 23g (Saturated Fat 9g, Trans Fat 1g); Cholesterol 115mg; Sodium 900mg; Total Carbohydrate 24g (Dietary Fiber 1g); Protein 38g **Exchanges:** 1½ Starch, 2 Lean Meat, 1½ Medium-Fat Meat, 1 High-Fat Meat **Carbohydrate Choices:** 1½

Love burgers and Asian food? Then this recipe is the best of both worlds! The tasty chicken burgers can be on and off the grill in just 25 minutes.

Prep Time:
25 Minutes

Start to Finish:
25 Minutes

4 burgers

Asian Chicken Burgers

1½	cups coleslaw mix (from 16-oz bag)	½	cup unseasoned dry bread crumbs
1	medium green onion, chopped (1 tablespoon)	1	tablespoon soy sauce
3	tablespoons Asian vinaigrette dressing	2	cloves garlic, finely chopped
		2	teaspoons sesame oil
1	lb ground chicken	¼	teaspoon freshly ground pepper
		4	burger buns, split

1 Heat gas or charcoal grill. In small bowl, toss coleslaw mix and onion with dressing; set aside.

2 In medium bowl, mix remaining ingredients except buns. Shape mixture into 4 patties, about ¾ inch thick.

3 Carefully brush oil on grill rack. Place patties on grill over medium heat. Cover grill; cook 10 to 14 minutes, turning once, until thermometer inserted in center of patties reads 165°F. During last 2 minutes of cooking, place buns, cut sides down, on grill.

4 Place burgers on bun bottoms. Using slotted spoon, top each burger with about ⅓ cup coleslaw mixture. Cover with bun tops.

1 Burger: Calories 360; Total Fat 15g (Saturated Fat 3.5g, Trans Fat 0g); Cholesterol 65mg; Sodium 610mg; Total Carbohydrate 35g (Dietary Fiber 2g); Protein 20g **Exchanges:** 2 Starch, ½ Other Carbohydrate, 2 Very Lean Meat, 2½ Fat **Carbohydrate Choices:** 2

> TRY THIS Add ¼ teaspoon ground ginger to the chicken mixture before shaping the patties.

> FRESH FACT Lean ground chicken is a tasty, healthy meat choice. Cook the patties until they are fully cooked (to 165°F on a meat thermometer), but don't overcook, as they dry out easily. Do not press the patties while cooking.

Looking for loads of flavor without loads of dishes? Try this full Southwest-inspired meal broiled in a single sheet pan.

Prep Time:
30 Minutes

Start to Finish:
30 Minutes

4 servings

Southwestern Steak with Corn and Chiles

2 tablespoons roasted salted hulled pumpkin seeds (pepitas), finely chopped	**4** ears fresh sweet corn, husks removed, cut in half crosswise, or 8 frozen small corn-on-the-cob
2 teaspoons Southwest seasoning blend	**2** large poblano chiles, cut in half lengthwise, stems and seeds removed
½ teaspoon pepper	**1** medium onion, cut into 8 wedges
1 lb boneless beef sirloin steak (1 inch thick)	**¼** cup roasted salted hulled pumpkin seeds (pepitas)
4 teaspoons olive oil	

1 In small bowl, mix 2 tablespoons chopped pumpkin seeds, 1 teaspoon of the seasoning blend and the pepper. Press mixture into all sides of beef; let stand at room temperature 15 minutes.

2 Meanwhile, set oven control to broil. Line 15x10x1-inch pan with heavy-duty foil; spray foil with cooking spray. In same small bowl, mix oil and remaining 1 teaspoon seasoning blend. Place corn, chiles and onion in pan. Drizzle oil mixture over vegetables; toss until evenly coated. Push vegetables together in single layer on sides of pan, leaving room in center for beef.

3 Broil 4 to 6 inches from heat 10 to 15 minutes for medium doneness (160°F), turning beef and vegetables halfway through cooking time.

4 Slice beef; place on serving plate. Add vegetables to plate; sprinkle with ¼ cup pumpkin seeds.

1 Serving: Calories 410; Total Fat 16g (Saturated Fat 3.5g, Trans Fat 0g); Cholesterol 80mg; Sodium 170mg; Total Carbohydrate 27g (Dietary Fiber 4g); Protein 39g **Exchanges:** 2 Starch, 4 Lean Meat, ½ High-Fat Meat **Carbohydrate Choices:** 2

> TRY THIS You can prepare and refrigerate this dinner up to 24 hours in advance. Making it ahead will allow more of the delicious flavors of the marinade to penetrate the beef and veggies. Then simply pop it in the oven, adding a few extra minutes to the cooking time.

Capture the flavor of gyros in these Greek-inspired beef burgers served in pita breads. They're a fun change from the typical hamburger and just as quick to grill!

Prep Time:
30 Minutes

Start to Finish:
30 Minutes

4 servings

Greek Burgers

1   **lb lean (at least 80%) ground beef**

½   **cup crumbled herb-flavored feta cheese (2 oz)**

¼   **cup chopped kalamata olives**

1   **tablespoon chopped fresh oregano leaves**

2   **teaspoons chopped fresh mint leaves**

4   **pita (pocket) breads (6 inch), cut in half to form pockets**

½   **medium cucumber, thinly sliced**

4   **thin slices red onion, cut in half**

1   **medium tomato, sliced**

¼   **cup fat-free Greek plain yogurt**

1   Heat gas or charcoal grill. In large bowl, mix beef, cheese, olives, oregano and mint. Shape mixture into 4 patties, about ½ inch thick.

2   Place patties on grill over medium heat. Cover grill; cook 10 to 12 minutes, turning once, until meat thermometer inserted in center of patties reads 160°F.

3   Cut burgers in half. Fill each pita pocket with burger half and cucumber, onion and tomato slices; drizzle with yogurt.

1 Serving: Calories 420; Total Fat 17g (Saturated Fat 7g, Trans Fat 1g); Cholesterol 85mg; Sodium 620mg; Total Carbohydrate 38g (Dietary Fiber 2g); Protein 29g **Exchanges:** 2½ Starch, 3 Medium-Fat Meat **Carbohydrate Choices:** 2½

> GO-WITH IDEA Serve with a Greek pasta salad and watermelon slices. Or, if you're really in a hurry, your favorite potato chips will do just fine!

Love grilled beef and southwestern food? Then you'll savor this mouthwatering 25-minute entrée. The cilantro-jalapeño relish takes steaks over the top.

Prep Time:
25 Minutes

Start to Finish:
25 Minutes

4 servings

Sirloin Steaks with Cilantro Chimichurri

1	cup loosely packed fresh cilantro	2	teaspoons oil
1	small onion, cut into quarters	1¼	teaspoons salt
2	cloves garlic, cut in half	2	teaspoons ground cumin
1	jalapeño chile, cut in half, seeded	½	teaspoon pepper
2	teaspoons lime juice	4	boneless beef sirloin steaks, 1 inch thick (about 1½ lb)

1 Heat gas or charcoal grill. In food processor, place cilantro, onion, garlic, chile, lime juice, oil and ¼ teaspoon of the salt. Cover; process until finely chopped. Blend in 2 to 3 teaspoons water to make chimichurri thinner, if desired. Transfer to small bowl; set aside until serving time.

2 In small bowl, mix cumin, pepper and remaining 1 teaspoon salt; rub evenly over steaks. Place steaks on grill over medium heat. Cover grill; cook 7 to 10 minutes for medium-rare doneness (145°F), turning once halfway through cooking.

3 Serve 2 tablespoons chimichurri with each steak.

1 Serving: Calories 290; Total Fat 9g (Saturated Fat 2.5g, Trans Fat 0g); Cholesterol 120mg; Sodium 800mg; Total Carbohydrate 3g (Dietary Fiber 0g); Protein 48g **Exchanges:** ½ Vegetable, 4½ Very Lean Meat, 2 Lean Meat **Carbohydrate Choices:** 0

> TRY THIS Substitute a serrano chile for the jalapeño, or add a pinch of ground red pepper (cayenne) if chiles are not available.

25 MINUTES OR LESS

Prep Time:
15 Minutes

Start to Finish:
25 Minutes

4 servings

Beef bites and three kinds of vegetables quickly cook in a grill basket for a hot and hearty appetizer, or a light meal, in 25 minutes.

Grilled Veggies and Steak

⅔ cup balsamic vinaigrette dressing

1 package (6 oz) small fresh portabella mushrooms

½ lb boneless beef sirloin steak (about ¾ inch thick), cut into ¾-inch cubes

1 cup frozen pearl onions, thawed

½ cup halved grape or cherry tomatoes

> **GO-WITH IDEA**
For a light and simple summertime meal, serve with a loaf of ciabatta or French bread and purchased tapenade.

1 Heat gas or charcoal grill. Reserve 2 tablespoons of the dressing. In large bowl, toss remaining dressing with mushrooms, beef and onions. Let stand 10 minutes; drain. Place mixture in grill basket (grill "wok").

2 Place basket on grill over medium-high heat. Cover grill; cook 7 to 9 minutes, shaking basket or stirring mixture twice, until vegetables are tender and beef is desired doneness. Stir in tomatoes.

3 Spoon beef mixture into serving dish. Stir in reserved dressing.

1 Serving: Calories 150; Total Fat 5g (Saturated Fat 1g, Trans Fat 0g); Cholesterol 30mg; Sodium 350mg; Total Carbohydrate 10g (Dietary Fiber 1g); Protein 15g **Exchanges:** 1 Vegetable, 2 Very Lean Meat, 1 Fat **Carbohydrate Choices:** ½

Heirloom Tomatoes

Heirloom tomatoes are hand-grown from seeds that have been passed down through generations. They have distinct attributes like exceptional flavor, unusual shapes and a wide range of colors. They are most commonly found at farmers' markets, June through August, in a variety of colors and sizes.

Unlike the grocery store varieties bred to withstand shipping and longer shelf lives, heirloom tomatoes are more delicate. Store them at room temperature, but out of direct sunlight. They should be used within three or four days of purchase.

Simply slice and eat these gorgeous fruits, perhaps with a light sprinkling of sea salt, or try one of the ideas below.

CAPRESE STACKS Layer sliced tomatoes with sliced mozzarella and fresh basil leaves. Drizzle with olive oil and balsamic vinegar.

HEIRLOOM TOMATO–ROASTED PEPPER PIZZA
On purchased pizza crust, arrange 2 or 3 varieties of sliced tomatoes. Top with 1 cup sliced roasted yellow bell peppers and ½ cup sliced ripe olives. Sprinkle with 1 cup shredded mozzarella cheese. Bake as directed on pizza crust package.

TOMATO AND PEACH SALAD On shallow platter, toss 2 cups diced tomatoes with 2 cups diced peaches and 1 cup cooked rotini pasta. Drizzle with ¼ cup balsamic dressing and 2 tablespoons chopped fresh basil.

PESTO-TOMATO BRUSCHETTA Spread French bread slices with refrigerated pesto (about 1 teaspoon per slice). Top with sliced prosciutto and tomato. Sprinkle with shredded Parmesan cheese and bake at 400°F for 3 to 5 minutes or until warm.

TOMATO NIÇOISE SALAD In medium serving dish, arrange 1 medium sliced cucumber with 2 sliced tomatoes with 8 ounces cooked fresh or canned tuna. Top with 1 chopped hard cooked-egg and drizzle with ¼ cup Italian dressing.

BABY GREENS WITH TOMATOES In large bowl, toss 3 cups mixed baby greens with 4 slices chopped, cooked bacon and 2 cups chopped tomatoes. Sprinkle with ½ cup crumbled blue cheese and drizzle with ¼ cup vinaigrette dressing.

Tender grilled pork—perfect for a main course that can be ready in 30 minutes! To round out the meal, serve with mashed sweet potatoes and sautéed apples.

Prep Time:
30 Minutes

Start to Finish:
30 Minutes

4 servings

Grilled Chili-Rubbed Pork Tenderloin

2 teaspoons packed brown sugar	⅛ teaspoon ground red pepper (cayenne)
1½ teaspoons chili powder	1 clove garlic, finely chopped
1 teaspoon salt	1 pork tenderloin (about 1 lb)
1 teaspoon ground cumin	1 teaspoon vegetable oil

1 Heat gas or charcoal grill. In small bowl, mix brown sugar, chili powder, salt, cumin, red pepper and garlic. Brush pork with oil. Rub and press spice mixture on all sides of pork.

2 Place pork on grill over medium heat. Cover grill; cook 17 to 20 minutes, turning several times, until meat thermometer inserted in center reads 145°F. Remove from grill. Cover; let stand 3 minutes before slicing.

1 Serving: Calories 170; Total Fat 6g (Saturated Fat 1.5g, Trans Fat 0g); Cholesterol 70mg; Sodium 650mg; Total Carbohydrate 3g (Dietary Fiber 0g); Protein 26g **Exchanges:** 3½ Very Lean Meat, 1 Fat **Carbohydrate Choices:** 0

> TRY THIS Imagine lively, seasoned butter melting over this tender grilled pork! Just mix up a little extra of the seasoning rub mixture and stir it into softened butter. Pass it around at the table.

Pair a spicy fruit salsa with zesty grilled pork chops and have it on your dinner table in less than 30 minutes.

Prep Time:
25 Minutes

Start to Finish:
25 Minutes

4 servings

Grilled Pork Chops with Peach Salsa

3 ripe medium peaches, peeled, chopped (about 1½ cups)

¼ cup finely chopped red bell pepper

2 tablespoons finely chopped red onion

1 tablespoon chopped fresh cilantro

2 teaspoons packed brown sugar

2 teaspoons fresh lime juice

¼ teaspoon finely chopped serrano or jalapeño chile

4 bone-in pork loin chops, ½ inch thick (1 lb)

1 tablespoon chili powder

1 Heat gas or charcoal grill. In medium bowl, mix peaches, bell pepper, onion, cilantro, brown sugar, lime juice and chile; set aside until serving time.

2 Rub both sides of pork chops with chili powder. Place pork on grill over medium heat. Cover grill; cook 6 to 9 minutes, turning once, until pork is no longer pink in center. Serve with salsa.

1 Serving: Calories 240; Total Fat 9g (Saturated Fat 3g, Trans Fat 0g); Cholesterol 65mg; Sodium 60mg; Total Carbohydrate 15g (Dietary Fiber 2g); Protein 24g **Exchanges:** 1 Other Carbohydrate, 3½ Very Lean Meat, 1½ Fat **Carbohydrate Choices:** 1

> TRY THIS If ripe peaches aren't available, substitute chopped mango or pineapple.

The sweet pepper mayo adds a spicy tang to these burgers—it's a fun twist on Cajun cuisine.

Prep Time:
25 Minutes

Start to Finish:
25 Minutes

4 burgers

Spicy Cajun Pork Burgers

SWEET PEPPER MAYO

2   tablespoons chopped drained sweet red piquante peppers (from 8- or 12-oz jar)

¼   cup mayonnaise

BURGERS

2   tablespoons chili sauce

¼   teaspoon Cajun seasoning

½   lb ground pork

½   lb bulk andouille or chorizo sausage

4   slices (1 oz each) Monterey Jack cheese

4   burger buns, split

4   small pieces leaf lettuce

1   Heat gas or charcoal grill. Pat chopped peppers with paper towels to remove excess moisture. In small bowl, mix mayonnaise and peppers; set aside.

2   In medium bowl, mix chili sauce and Cajun seasoning. Crumble pork and sausage into chili sauce mixture; mix gently just until combined. Shape mixture into 4 patties, about ½ inch thick.

3   Place patties on grill over medium heat. Cover grill; cook 6 to 10 minutes, turning once, until thermometer inserted in center of patties reads 160°F. During last 2 minutes of cooking, top each patty with cheese. Cook until cheese is melted.

4   Spread sweet pepper mayo on cut sides of buns. On bun bottoms, place lettuce and burgers; cover with bun tops.

1 Burger: Calories 700; Total Fat 51g (Saturated Fat 18g, Trans Fat 0.5g); Cholesterol 120mg; Sodium 1370mg; Total Carbohydrate 25g (Dietary Fiber 1g); Protein 36g **Exchanges:** 1½ Starch, 2½ Medium-Fat Meat, 2 High-Fat Meat, 4½ Fat **Carbohydrate Choices:** 1½

> FRESH FACT Sweet red piquante peppers are bright red and described as a cross between a red bell pepper and a ripe tomato. They are often sold at olive bars in the supermarket, in addition to being available in jars. If you can't find them, substitute sweet cherry peppers (from a 12- or 16-ounce jar), chopped, or even sweet pickle relish.

Five ingredients and 20 minutes are all you need to serve up these mouthwatering pork burgers! A slice of grilled pineapple adds a tropical touch.

Prep Time:
20 Minutes

Start to Finish:
20 Minutes

4 burgers

Pineapple Pork Burgers

1   **lb ground pork**
2   **tablespoons dry applewood rub seasoning**

1   **can (8 oz) pineapple slices in juice, drained, 2 tablespoons juice reserved**
4   **onion or plain burger buns, split**
4   **leaves leaf lettuce**

1   Heat gas or charcoal grill. In medium bowl, mix pork, seasoning and 2 tablespoons reserved pineapple juice. Shape mixture into 4 patties, about ½ inch thick.

2   Place patties on grill over medium heat. Cover grill; cook 6 to 7 minutes, turning once, until no longer pink in center and meat thermometer inserted in center of patties reads 160°F. During last 4 minutes of cooking, add pineapple slices to grill, turning once.

3   On each bun bottom, place lettuce, burger and pineapple slice. Cover with bun tops.

1 Burger: Calories 380; Total Fat 18g (Saturated Fat 6g, Trans Fat 0g); Cholesterol 70mg; Sodium 630mg; Total Carbohydrate 31g (Dietary Fiber 2g); Protein 24g **Exchanges:** 1 Starch, ½ Fruit, ½ Other Carbohydrate, ½ Vegetable, 1½ Lean Meat, 1½ Medium-Fat Meat, 1 Fat **Carbohydrate Choices:** 2

> TRY THIS Grill a few extra pineapple slices and save in the refrigerator to add to chicken salad another time.

Break the plain pork tenderloin routine with a spicy Asian sauce served alongside. Wasabi powder adds a fun kick.

Prep Time:
30 Minutes

Start to Finish:
30 Minutes

4 servings

Ginger Pork with Wasabi Aioli

PORK

2	**teaspoons ground ginger**
½	**teaspoon salt**
½	**teaspoon pepper**
1	**pork tenderloin (about 1 lb)**
1	**teaspoon vegetable oil**

AIOLI

¼	**cup mayonnaise**
2	**teaspoons wasabi powder**
1	**clove garlic, finely chopped**

1 Heat gas or charcoal grill. In small bowl, mix ginger, salt and pepper. Brush pork with oil; rub and press ginger mixture on all sides of pork.

2 Place pork on grill over medium heat. Cover grill; cook 17 to 20 minutes, turning several times, until meat thermometer inserted in center reads 145°F. Remove from grill. Cover; let stand 3 minutes.

3 Meanwhile, in small bowl, mix aioli ingredients. Cut pork into thin slices; serve with aioli.

1 Serving: Calories 250; Total Fat 17g (Saturated Fat 3.5g, Trans Fat 0g); Cholesterol 55mg; Sodium 430mg; Total Carbohydrate 2g (Dietary Fiber 0g); Protein 22g **Exchanges:** 3 Lean Meat, 1½ Fat **Carbohydrate Choices:** 0

> GO-WITH IDEA Serve with hot, cooked rice, stir-fried vegetables and sliced fresh pineapple.

> TRY THIS The wasabi aioli also makes a terrific sandwich spread.

Enjoy this apricot preserves and vinegar-marinated grilled pork chop and veggies recipe, for dinner that's ready in just 30 minutes. Serve over hot, cooked rice!

Prep Time:
30 Minutes

Start to Finish:
30 Minutes

4 servings
(2 kabobs each)

Pork Kabobs

4	boneless pork loin chops, ½ to ¾ inch thick (1 lb), trimmed of fat
½	teaspoon seasoned salt or pork seasoning
2	small zucchini, each cut into 8 pieces

16	medium mushrooms
1	medium red bell pepper, cut into 16 pieces
½	cup apricot preserves
1	tablespoon cider vinegar

1. Heat gas or charcoal grill. Sprinkle both sides of pork chops with seasoned salt; cut each chop into 4 pieces.

2. On 8 (8-inch) metal skewers, alternately thread pork, zucchini, mushrooms and bell pepper, leaving about ¼-inch space between each piece. In small bowl, mix preserves and vinegar.

3. Place kabobs on grill over medium heat. Brush with half of preserves mixture. Cook uncovered 5 minutes. Turn kabobs; brush with remaining preserves mixture. Cook 5 to 7 minutes longer or until pork is no longer pink.

1 Serving: Calories 320; Total Fat 9g (Saturated Fat 3g, Trans Fat 0g); Cholesterol 70mg; Sodium 230mg; Total Carbohydrate 33g (Dietary Fiber 2g); Protein 26g **Exchanges:** 1½ Other Carbohydrate, 2½ Vegetable, 3 Lean Meat **Carbohydrate Choices:** 2

> TRY THIS Kabobs can be broiled instead of grilled. Set oven control to broil. Assemble kabobs as directed and place on broiler pan; brush with half of preserves mixture. Broil 4 to 6 inches from heat about 10 to 12 minutes, turning once and brushing with remaining preserves mixture.

Enjoy these herbed lamb chops grilled to perfection—a mouth-watering meal elegant enough for company, that can be easily doubled or tripled.

Prep Time:
20 Minutes

Start to Finish:
20 Minutes

2 servings
(3 chops each)

Grilled Rosemary Lamb Chops

1   tablespoon country-style Dijon mustard

1   tablespoon chopped fresh rosemary leaves

2   teaspoons honey

1   clove garlic, finely chopped

½   teaspoon salt

¼   teaspoon coarse ground black pepper

6   French-cut baby lamb chops (1 to 1¼ inches thick)

1 Heat gas or charcoal grill. In small bowl, mix all ingredients except lamb. Spread mixture on one side of each lamb chop.

2 Place lamb, coated side up, on grill over medium heat. Cover grill; cook 12 to 15 minutes for medium doneness (160°F).

1 Serving: Calories 330; Total Fat 14g (Saturated Fat 5g, Trans Fat 0.5g); Cholesterol 140mg; Sodium 880mg; Total Carbohydrate 7g (Dietary Fiber 0g); Protein 43g **Exchanges:** ½ Other Carbohydrate, 6 Very Lean Meat, 2 Fat **Carbohydrate Choices:** ½

> FRESH FACT French-cut lamb chops are small and very tender. If these chops are not available, the recipe can also be made with lamb loin or sirloin chops. Both of these cuts will be a little meatier, so plan on 1 or 2 chops per serving.

> GO WITH IDEA Serve the chops with parsley-buttered new potatoes and a tossed mixed greens salad.

Grilled salmon gets a simple yet tasty treatment in this four-ingredient, 20-minute recipe.

Prep Time:
20 Minutes

Start to Finish:
20 Minutes

4 servings

Crispy-Coated Lemon-Pepper Salmon

¼ **cup buttermilk**

3 **tablespoons butter, melted**

½ **cup lemon pepper panko crispy bread crumbs**

1 **salmon fillet (1½ lb), cut into 4 serving pieces**

1 Heat gas or charcoal grill. In shallow dish, place buttermilk. In small bowl, mix butter and bread crumbs. Dip salmon in buttermilk. Press crumb mixture evenly on top of salmon pieces.

2 Carefully brush oil on grill rack. Place salmon, skin side down, on grill over medium heat. Cover grill; cook 10 to 14 minutes or until fish flakes easily with fork.

1 Serving: Calories 380; Total Fat 21g (Saturated Fat 8g, Trans Fat 0g); Cholesterol 135mg; Sodium 390mg; Total Carbohydrate 9g (Dietary Fiber 0g); Protein 38g **Exchanges:** ½ Starch, 5½ Lean Meat, 1 Fat **Carbohydrate Choices:** ½

> **GO-WITH IDEA** Serve with lemon wedges and either a fresh red onion and cucumber salad, or cooked fresh asparagus and a couscous salad.

> **TRY THIS** Use a metal turner to lift the salmon from the grill with the skin attached or carefully lift away from the skin to serve.

Grilled and drizzled with a tangy vinaigrette, mussels make an out-of-the-ordinary entrée that is easy to double or triple for larger groups.

Prep Time:
25 Minutes

Start to Finish:
25 Minutes

2 servings

Grilled Mussels with Spanish-Style Vinaigrette

24 large fresh mussels in shells (2 lb)	1 tablespoon diced pimientos, drained
⅓ cup olive or vegetable oil	1 teaspoon capers, if desired
3 tablespoons red wine vinegar or sherry vinegar	¼ teaspoon salt
1 tablespoon chopped fresh parsley	6 drops red pepper sauce
	1 green onion, finely chopped

1 Discard any broken-shell or open (dead) mussels that do not close when tapped. Scrub remaining mussels, removing any barnacles with a dull paring knife. Remove beards by tugging them away from shells.

2 Place mussels in large container. Cover with cool water. Agitate water with hand, then drain and discard water. Repeat several times until water runs clear; drain.

3 Heat gas or charcoal grill. In tightly covered container, shake remaining ingredients. Cover; refrigerate until serving time.

4 Place mussels on grill over medium-high heat. Cover grill; cook 5 to 7 minutes or until mussels open, removing mussels as they open. Discard any unopened mussels. Place mussels on serving platter; drizzle with oil mixture.

1 Serving: Calories 420; Total Fat 37g (Saturated Fat 5g, Trans Fat 0g); Cholesterol 45mg; Sodium 680mg; Total Carbohydrate 4g (Dietary Fiber 0g); Protein 17g **Exchanges:** 2½ Lean Meat, 6 Fat **Carbohydrate Choices:** 0

> GO-WITH IDEA The mussels are great served with corn on the cob and crusty bread.

Trying to eat more fish? These steaks, topped with a corn and tomato relish, are a perfect weeknight dinner.

Prep Time:
25 Minutes

Start to Finish:
25 Minutes

4 servings

Cajun Halibut

CORN RELISH

- **1** **can (7 oz) whole kernel corn, drained**
- **1** **medium plum (Roma) tomato, chopped (⅓ cup)**
- **2** **medium green onions, chopped (2 tablespoons)**
- **1** **tablespoon cider vinegar**
- **2** **teaspoons honey**
- **¾** **teaspoon dried oregano leaves**

- **¼** **teaspoon ground red pepper (cayenne)**
- **¼** **teaspoon salt**

FISH

- **4** **halibut steaks (about 6 oz each)**
- **2** **tablespoons Worcestershire sauce**
- **½** **teaspoon coarse ground black pepper**
- **¼** **teaspoon dried oregano leaves**

1 Heat gas or charcoal grill. In small bowl, mix corn relish ingredients; set aside until serving time.

2 Brush halibut with Worcestershire sauce; sprinkle with black pepper and ¼ teaspoon oregano.

3 Place halibut on grill over medium heat. Cover grill; cook 10 to 15 minutes, turning once or twice, until fish flakes easily with fork. Serve with corn relish.

1 Serving: Calories 220; Total Fat 2.5g (Saturated Fat 0.5g, Trans Fat 0g); Cholesterol 90mg; Sodium 520mg; Total Carbohydrate 15g (Dietary Fiber 1g); Protein 33g **Exchanges:** ½ Starch, ½ Other Carbohydrate, 4½ Very Lean Meat **Carbohydrate Choices:** 1

CHAPTER 5

Fruit and Veggie Sides

15 MINUTES OR LESS

Prep Time:
15 Minutes

Start to Finish:
15 Minutes

4 servings

Pull this elegant salad together quickly with the help of a microwave and a handful of flavorful ingredients that complement each other gorgeously.

Beet and Baby Greens Salad

4   small red or gold beets, stems removed, peeled and cut into ¼-inch slices (about 2 cups)

¼   cup olive oil

3   tablespoons balsamic vinegar

4   cups mixed baby salad greens

½   cup chopped red onion

½   cup crumbled feta cheese (2 oz)

1   In 9-inch microwavable pie plate, place beets, overlapping slightly. Add ¼ cup water; cover with microwavable plastic wrap. Microwave on High 4 to 5 minutes or until almost tender when pierced with fork; drain.

2   In small bowl, beat oil and vinegar with whisk until blended. Divide salad greens among 4 plates; top with beets. Drizzle evenly with dressing; sprinkle with onion and cheese.

1 Serving: Calories 230; Total Fat 17g (Saturated Fat 4g, Trans Fat 0g); Cholesterol 15mg; Sodium 240mg; Total Carbohydrate 14g (Dietary Fiber 4g); Protein 4g **Exchanges:** ½ Other Carbohydrate, 1 Vegetable, ½ Medium-Fat Meat, 3 Fat **Carbohydrate Choices:** 1

> FRESH FACT If your beets are large, cut them in half, then cut into ¼-inch slices. If using both red and gold beets, microwave them with the red on one side of the pie plate and the gold on the other, so just a little of the red color leeches onto the gold beets. If the two colors are arranged randomly, the gold beets will all become red.

Beets

There's no mistaking the beautiful hue of golden-yellow and rich, red beets. Their notable earthy flavor plays well with bright flavors like orange and the tangy taste of fresh goat cheese. One of the most popular ways to enjoy them is roasted. To roast beets, cut off most of the stem end but leave the root ends attached. Brush with a little olive oil and wrap in foil. Place in a shallow pan and roast at 425°F for 35 to 45 minutes or until fork-tender.

Because beets are in season year-round, they're easy to find. Look for bright-colored, firm beets with smooth skins—and be sure to check out the milder-flavored golden variety if you have an opportunity. Greens should be removed as soon as possible and stored separately. To store beets, refrigerate in a plastic bag for up to one week.

Here are some tasty ways to use roasted beets.

ORANGE-GLAZED BEETS In medium saucepan, cook 1 teaspoon grated orange peel, ½ cup orange juice and 2 tablespoons packed brown sugar. Cook and stir 3 to 4 minutes or until bubbly. Stir in 2 cups diced roasted beets. Cook 4 to 5 minutes or until hot and glazed.

ROASTED BEET SALAD For each salad, place 1 cup mixed baby greens on a salad plate. Top with ½ to 1 cup sliced roasted beets, 2 to 3 orange slices, 1 tablespoon chopped walnuts and 2 tablespoons crumbled chèvre (goat) cheese. Drizzle with herb vinaigrette dressing.

SOUR CREAM AND DILL BEETS Slice 2 cups cooled, roasted beets and place in shallow serving bowl. Top with ½ cup sour cream and 1 to 2 tablespoons fresh chopped dill.

BLUE CHEESE–PECAN BEETS Cut roasted beets into wedges or cubes to measure 2 cups and place in shallow serving bowl. Toss with 1 to 2 tablespoons each olive oil and balsamic vinegar. Sprinkle with ½ cup crumbled blue cheese and ¼ cup pecan halves.

QUICK BEET STIR-FRY In 10-inch skillet, heat 1 tablespoon olive oil. Cook 1 cup julienne-cut carrots and ½ cup julienne-cut green bell pepper just until fork-tender. Stir in 1½ cups julienne-cut roasted beets, 1 tablespoon chopped fresh tarragon or marjoram and 1 tablespoon orange or lemon juice. Cook and stir just until hot.

BUTTERY BABY BEETS In 10-inch skillet, melt 2 tablespoons butter over medium heat. Stir in 2 cups roasted baby beets; sprinkle with ¼ teaspoon each salt and coarse ground black pepper and 2 tablespoons chopped fresh chives. Cook 2 to 3 minutes or just until hot.

Salad Lyonnaise is a gorgeous classic salad that includes soft-cooked eggs and bacon. The spicy vinaigrette dressing is a perfect topping for this elegant salad.

Prep Time:
20 Minutes

Start to Finish:
20 Minutes

4 servings

Salad Lyonnaise

RED WINE VINAIGRETTE DRESSING

- 3 **tablespoons olive oil**
- 1 **tablespoon red wine vinegar**
- 2 **teaspoons Dijon mustard**
- 1 **teaspoon finely chopped shallot**
- ½ **teaspoon sugar**
- ⅛ **teaspoon coarse ground black pepper**

SALAD

- 4 **eggs**
- 6 **cups torn frisée or escarole**
- 4 **slices bacon, crisply cooked, crumbled**
- ¾ **cup herb or garlic croutons**

  Additional coarse ground black pepper, if desired

  Paprika, if desired

1 In small bowl, mix dressing ingredients with whisk until smooth. Refrigerate until serving time.

2 In skillet or saucepan (large enough so eggs do not touch during cooking), heat 2 to 3 inches water to boiling; reduce heat so water is simmering. Break cold egg into custard cup. Holding cup close to water's surface, carefully slide egg into water. Repeat with a second egg. Cook uncovered 3 to 5 minutes or until whites and yolks are firm, not runny. Remove eggs with slotted spoon; cover to keep warm. Repeat with remaining 2 eggs.

3 Stir dressing. In large bowl, toss frisée and dressing until coated. Divide among 4 shallow bowls or plates. Top each with poached egg, bacon and croutons. Sprinkle egg with pepper and paprika.

1 Serving: Calories 230; Total Fat 20g (Saturated Fat 4.5g, Trans Fat 0g); Cholesterol 195mg; Sodium 290mg; Total Carbohydrate 4g (Dietary Fiber 1g); Protein 10g **Exchanges:** 1 Vegetable, 1 Medium-Fat Meat, 3 Fat **Carbohydrate Choices:** 0

> TRY THIS You can fry the eggs rather than poaching them, if desired.

Classic Greek salad makes a beautiful accompaniment or start to so many meals. Want to make it a meal in itself? Add some grilled and sliced chicken breast to this flavorful salad.

Prep Time:
20 Minutes

Start to Finish:
20 Minutes

8 servings
(1¾ cups)

Greek Salad

LEMON DRESSING

- ¼ **cup olive oil**
- 2 **tablespoons fresh lemon juice**
- 1½ **teaspoons Dijon mustard**
- ½ **teaspoon sugar**
- ¼ **teaspoon salt**
- ⅛ **teaspoon pepper**

SALAD

- 5 **cups fresh baby spinach leaves**
- 1 **head Boston lettuce, torn into bite-size pieces (4 cups)**
- 1 **cup crumbled feta cheese**
- 24 **pitted kalamata or Greek olives**
- 4 **medium green onions, sliced (¼ cups)**
- 3 **medium tomatoes, cut into wedges**
- 1 **medium cucumber, sliced**

1 In tightly covered container, shake all dressing ingredients. In large bowl, toss salad ingredients and dressing. Serve immediately.

1 Serving: Calories 140; Total Fat 11g (Saturated Fat 3.5g, Trans Fat 0g); Sodium 680mg; Total Carbohydrate 6g (Dietary Fiber 2g); Protein 4g **Exchanges:** 1 Vegetable, 2½ Fat **Carbohydrate Choices:** ½

> TRY THIS You can substitute extra-large ripe olives for the kalamata olives, or chopped red onion in place of the sliced green onions.

This Middle Eastern salad is bursting with fresh flavors. Pita bread on the side continues the flavors and makes a great go-to. For a variation, don't break up the pita breads and instead eat the salad inside the pita pockets.

Prep Time:
25 Minutes

Start to Finish:
25 Minutes

4 servings

Fattoush Salad

¾   **cup fresh lemon juice**

¼   **cup olive oil**

¼   **teaspoon salt**

½   **teaspoon pepper**

4   **cloves garlic, finely chopped**

1   **cup diced unpeeled hothouse (seedless) cucumber**

3   **plum (Roma) tomatoes, diced (1¾ cups)**

½   **red bell pepper, diced (½ cup)**

3   **cups thinly sliced red cabbage**

½   **cup chopped fresh Italian (flat-leaf) parsley**

¼   **cup chopped fresh mint leaves**

2   **pita (pocket) breads (6 inch), toasted, torn into 1-inch chunks**

1   In large bowl, beat lemon juice, oil, salt, pepper and garlic with whisk. Add remaining ingredients except pita; toss well to combine.

2   Divide salad among 4 shallow bowls or plates. Top with pita pieces.

1 Serving: Calories 250; Total Fat 14g (Saturated Fat 2g, Trans Fat 0g); Cholesterol 0mg; Sodium 290mg; Total Carbohydrate 25g (Dietary Fiber 3g); Protein 4g **Exchanges:** 1 Other Carbohydrate, 1½ Vegetable, 3 Fat **Carbohydrate Choices:** 1½

> FRESH FACT Hothouse cucumbers are also called English cucumbers. They have a sweeter flavor and are longer and thinner than regular cucumbers. Any seeds are tiny and very tender. The skin is also tender, so they don't require peeling.

> TIME-SAVER As a convenient alternative to squeezing fresh lemons, look for the bright yellow plastic bottles of frozen fresh lemon juice (7.5 ounces) in the freezer aisle or produce section of your grocery store.

Prep Time:
20 Minutes

Start to Finish:
20 Minutes

4 servings

Massaging kale removes some of the bite of this green and renders it much milder and more tender, but still packed with nutrients. Hearty kale greens work beautifully with strong flavors, such as vinaigrettes, and bold cheeses, such as blue.

Cherry-Walnut Kale Salad

1	bunch (8 oz) fresh kale, ribs removed, leaves thinly sliced (6 cups)	1	tablespoon honey
3	tablespoons fresh lemon juice	½	teaspoon pepper
1	tablespoon olive oil	2	tablespoons dried tart cherries
½	teaspoon salt	2	tablespoons chopped walnuts, toasted if desired
1	tablespoon white balsamic or white wine vinegar	2	tablespoons crumbled blue cheese

1 In large bowl, mix kale, lemon juice, 1 teaspoon of the oil and the salt. Massage kale with your hands 3 to 5 minutes or until it starts to wilt; set aside.

2 In small bowl, beat vinegar, honey and pepper with whisk. Slowly pour in remaining 2 teaspoons oil while continuing to beat. Pour dressing over kale mixture; toss to coat.

3 Top individual servings with cherries, walnuts and cheese.

1 Serving: Calories 120; Total Fat 5g (Saturated Fat 1.5g, Trans Fat 0g); Cholesterol 0mg; Sodium 380mg; Total Carbohydrate 16g (Dietary Fiber 1g); Protein 3g **Exchanges:** ½ Starch, 1 Vegetable, 1 Fat **Carbohydrate Choices:** 1

> **FRESH FACT** As an alternative to massaging kale, toss the leaves with oil, lemon juice and salt and refridgerate overnight.

Pack this multi-bean salad for your next picnic; the salad will stand up beautifully and features the creaminess of cannellini beans and the crunch of lightly cooked green and yellow beans.

Prep Time:
20 Minutes

Start to Finish:
20 Minutes

10 servings

Green and Yellow Bean Salad

SALAD

- **8** oz fresh green beans, trimmed
- **8** oz fresh yellow wax beans, trimmed
- **1** cup grape tomatoes, cut in half
- **1** can (15 oz) cannellini beans, drained, rinsed
- **¼** cup lightly packed fresh basil leaves, torn

SHERRY VINAIGRETTE DRESSING

- **¼** cup olive oil
- **2** tablespoons sherry vinegar
- **½** teaspoon salt
- **¼** teaspoon coarse ground black pepper

1 In 2-quart saucepan, place green and wax beans in 1 inch water. Heat to boiling; reduce heat. Simmer uncovered 8 to 10 minutes or until beans are crisp-tender. Rinse with cold water; drain.

2 In medium bowl, stir together cooked beans, tomatoes, cannellini beans and basil.

3 In jar with tight-fitting lid, shake dressing ingredients. Pour over salad; toss to coat.

1 Serving: Calories 110; Total Fat 6g (Saturated Fat 1g, Trans Fat 0g); Cholesterol 0mg; Sodium 220mg; Total Carbohydrate 12g (Dietary Fiber 3g); Protein 4g **Exchanges:** ½ Other Carbohydrate, ½ Vegetable, ½ Very Lean Meat, 1 Fat **Carbohydrate Choices:** 1

> TRY THIS The salad can be refrigerated at least 1 hour before serving, which will allow the flavors to blend. Stir before serving.

Heirloom tomatoes are beautiful to look at and more flavorful to eat than their hybrid grocery store companions. Try this fresh and classic Italian favorite, and then turn to page 185 for more ideas using heirloom tomatoes.

Prep Time:
10 Minutes

Start to Finish:
10 Minutes

8 servings

Heirloom Tomato Caprese Salad

2   containers (8 oz each) bocconcini (small fresh mozzarella cheese balls), drained

4   medium to large heirloom tomatoes, cut into wedges or slices

2   tablespoons balsamic vinegar

1   tablespoon olive oil

Coarse sea salt, flaked salt or colored salt, if desired

Freshly ground pepper, if desired

6   large fresh basil leaves, cut into thin strips

1   On serving platter, arrange cheese and tomatoes. Drizzle with vinegar and oil; sprinkle with salt and pepper. Sprinkle with basil. Serve immediately.

1 Serving: Calories 170; Total Fat 12g (Saturated Fat 0g, Trans Fat 0g); Cholesterol 40mg; Sodium 170mg; Total Carbohydrate 5g (Dietary Fiber 0g); Protein 10g **Exchanges:** ½ Vegetable, 1 Lean Meat, 2 Fat **Carbohydrate Choices:** ½

> **FRESH FACT** Basil leaves cut into thin strips are called "chiffonade." To cut, stack the leaves on top of each other, then roll up. Slice across the roll to form long shreds.

> **TRY THIS** If you want to splurge with ingredients, buy balsamic vinegar aged over 20 years. It has a syrupy consistency and a heavenly sweet and tangy flavor.

Crunchy veggies get a hearty protein boost from everyone's favorite combination, bacon and cheese, in this rich and creamy side dish.

Prep Time:
20 Minutes

Start to Finish:
20 Minutes

16 servings
(½ cup each)

Cauliflower Salad

10 slices bacon, cut into ½-inch pieces	1 small onion, finely chopped
1 cup mayonnaise or salad dressing	1 small green bell pepper, finely chopped
¼ cup sugar	8 oz Colby-Monterey Jack cheese blend, cut into ½-inch cubes
1 medium head cauliflower (about 2 lb), separated into florets	

1 In 12-inch nonstick skillet, cook bacon pieces over medium heat 5 to 7 minutes or until crisp. Drain on paper towels; set aside.

2 In large bowl, stir together mayonnaise and sugar. Stir in cauliflower, onion and bell pepper until vegetables are coated.

3 Just before serving, stir in cheese. Sprinkle with bacon.

1 Serving: Calories 210; Total Fat 17g (Saturated Fat 5g, Trans Fat 0g); Cholesterol 25mg; Sodium 280mg; Total Carbohydrate 6g (Dietary Fiber 1g); Protein 6g **Exchanges:** 1½ Vegetable, ½ High-Fat Meat, 2½ Fat **Carbohydrate Choices:** ½

> TIME-SAVER Make this recipe even speedier by using packaged precooked bacon. It's sold near the regular bacon and just needs to be heated in the microwave.

You can chop this salad yourself from fresh fruit, but if you want a super-speedy side, pick up some fresh fruit salad at the deli and you're five minutes from a refreshing side or dessert.

Prep Time:
5 Minutes

Start to Finish:
5 Minutes

8 servings
(1 cup each)

Speedy Honey-Lime Fruit Salad

½ cup refrigerated coleslaw dressing

3 tablespoons honey

1 teaspoon grated lime peel

1½ teaspoons fresh lime juice

8 cups fresh fruit salad (from deli)

1 In small bowl, mix dressing, honey, lime peel and lime juice until well blended.

2 Just before serving, in large bowl, gently mix fruit salad and dressing mixture to coat.

1 Serving: Calories 200; Total Fat 6g (Saturated Fat 1g, Trans Fat 0g); Cholesterol 5mg; Sodium 105mg; Total Carbohydrate 34g (Dietary Fiber 3g); Protein 1g **Exchanges:** 1 Fruit, 1½ Other Carbohydrate, 1 Fat **Carbohydrate Choices:** 2

Ten minutes and one step is all you need to wrap up this salad made using mixed greens and fruit, drizzled with vinaigrette.

Mixed Greens with Fruit and Raspberry Dressing

2 cups torn mixed salad greens

1 can (8 oz) pineapple tidbits, drained

1 cup fresh raspberries

2 medium bananas, sliced

2 medium green onions, sliced
(2 tablespoons)

½ cup fat-free raspberry
vinaigrette dressing

1 Divide salad greens among 4 plates; top evenly with pineapple, raspberries, bananas and onions. Drizzle each salad with 2 tablespoons dressing.

1 Serving: Calories 150; Total Fat 0.5g (Saturated Fat 0g, Trans Fat 0g); Cholesterol 0mg; Sodium 250mg; Total Carbohydrate 35g (Dietary Fiber 5g); Protein 2g **Exchanges:** 1 Fruit, 1½ Other Carbohydrate **Carbohydrate Choices:** 2

> TRY THIS To make a main-dish salad, top with a grilled chicken breast or several strips of leftover roast beef.

15 MINUTES OR LESS

The bite of gorgonzola and the crunchy sweetness of apple complement each other perfectly in this refined salad.

Prep Time:
15 Minutes

Start to Finish:
15 Minutes

6 servings

Apple-Gorgonzola Salad

RED WINE VINAIGRETTE DRESSING

- ⅓ cup olive or vegetable oil
- ¼ cup red wine vinegar
- 2 tablespoons sugar
- 1 teaspoon Dijon mustard
- 1 clove garlic, finely chopped

SALAD

- 1 bag (10 oz) mixed baby salad greens or Italian-blend (romaine and radicchio) salad greens
- 1 medium red or green apple, chopped (1 cup)
- ½ cup crumbled Gorgonzola or blue cheese (2 oz)
- ⅓ cup chopped walnuts, toasted*

1 In small bowl, beat dressing ingredients with whisk until smooth.

2 In large bowl, combine salad ingredients and toss with dressing just before serving.

*To toast walnuts, sprinkle in ungreased skillet. Cook over medium heat 5 to 7 minutes, stirring frequently until nuts begin to brown, then stirring constantly until nuts are light brown.

1 Serving: Calories 230; Total Fat 19g (Saturated Fat 4g, Trans Fat 0g); Cholesterol 5mg; Sodium 170mg; Total Carbohydrate 10g (Dietary Fiber 2g); Protein 4g **Exchanges:** ½ Other Carbohydrate, ½ High-Fat Meat, 3 Fat **Carbohydrate Choices:** ½

15 MINUTES OR LESS

A zesty mustard glaze adds a flavorful pop to colorful asparagus and corn. Cooking the vegetables before assembling the salad means that the warm asparagus and corn will absorb more of the dressing's flavor.

Prep Time:
15 Minutes

Start to Finish:
15 Minutes

5 servings
(½ cup each)

Asparagus and Corn with Honey-Mustard Glaze

1   lb fresh asparagus spears, trimmed, cut into 1-inch pieces

1   cup frozen whole kernel corn

2   teaspoons Dijon mustard

2   teaspoons honey

¼   teaspoon lemon-pepper seasoning

1 In 2-quart saucepan, heat ½ cup water to boiling. Add asparagus and corn; reduce heat. Simmer uncovered 5 to 8 minutes or until asparagus is crisp-tender; drain.

2 In small bowl, mix mustard, honey and lemon-pepper seasoning. Stir into vegetables.

1 Serving: Calories 60; Total Fat 0g (Saturated Fat 0g, Trans Fat 0g); Cholesterol 0mg; Sodium 70mg; Total Carbohydrate 12g (Dietary Fiber 2g); Protein 3g **Exchanges:** ½ Other Carbohydrate, 1 Vegetable **Carbohydrate Choices:** 1

> TRY THIS Green beans, cut into 1-inch pieces, can be substituted for the asparagus.

Serve a sensational side that's super simple! This interesting combination of broccoli and butternut squash is great for a crowd.

Prep Time:
25 Minutes

Start to Finish:
25 Minutes

14 servings
(½ cup each)

Broccoli and Squash Medley

2	bags (12 oz each) frozen cut broccoli	½	cup sweetened dried cranberries
2	cups cubed (½ inch) peeled butternut squash (1½ lb)	½	cup finely chopped pecans, toasted*
½	cup orange juice	1	tablespoon grated orange peel
¼	cup butter, melted	1	teaspoon salt

1 Cook and drain broccoli as directed on bag. Meanwhile, in 12-inch skillet, cook squash in orange juice over medium-low heat 8 to 10 minutes, stirring frequently, until tender but firm.

2 Add cooked broccoli and remaining ingredients to squash mixture; toss to coat. Serve immediately.

*To toast pecans, sprinkle in ungreased skillet. Cook over medium heat 5 to 7 minutes, stirring frequently until nuts begin to brown, then stirring constantly until nuts are light brown.

1 Serving: Calories 110; Total Fat 6g (Saturated Fat 2.5g, Trans Fat 0g); Cholesterol 10mg; Sodium 210mg; Total Carbohydrate 12g (Dietary Fiber 2g); Protein 2g **Exchanges:** 1 Starch, 1 Fat **Carbohydrate Choices:** 1

> TRY THIS Use your favorite nut in place of the pecans and swap out the cranberries for raisins, golden raisins or chopped dried apricots.

Garlic salt and fresh chives are all you need to flavor naturally delicious vegetables in a 20-minute side dish. This dish pairs wonderfully with chicken, as shown here.

Garden Patch Sauté

1 tablespoon olive or vegetable oil

1 medium zucchini, cut into ¼-inch slices (1 cup)

1 medium yellow summer squash, cut into ¼-inch slices (1 cup)

1 cup sliced fresh mushrooms (3 oz)

1 cup grape or cherry tomatoes, cut in half

2 tablespoons chopped fresh chives

½ teaspoon garlic salt

1 In 10-inch nonstick skillet, heat oil over medium-high heat. Cook zucchini, yellow squash and mushrooms in oil 4 to 5 minutes, stirring frequently, until squash is crisp-tender.

2 Stir in tomatoes. Sprinkle with chives and garlic salt. Cook 2 to 3 minutes, stirring frequently, just until tomatoes begin to soften.

1 Serving: Calories 40; Total Fat 2.5g (Saturated Fat 0g, Trans Fat 0g); Cholesterol 0mg; Sodium 85mg; Total Carbohydrate 3g (Dietary Fiber 1g); Protein 1g **Exchanges:** ½ Vegetable, ½ Fat **Carbohydrate Choices:** 0

> **TIME-SAVER** All of the vegetables and the chives can be cut a day ahead and kept covered in the refrigerator until you're ready to cook.

> **TRY THIS** Fresh basil, oregano, marjoram or even lemon balm can be substituted for the chives.

Spiralized vegetables are a great way to get the feel of noodles without the carbs or calories. A simple dressing of good olive oil and salt is all these spiralized veggies need to shine!

Prep Time:
10 Minutes

Start to Finish:
20 Minutes

4 servings

Spiral Summer Squash

1	zucchini (6 inches)	2	teaspoons olive oil
1	yellow summer squash (6 inches)	¼	teaspoon salt

1 Heat oven to 400°F. Line 15x10x1-inch pan with foil.

2 Cut off ends of squash. Cut squash with spiralizer according to manufacturer's directions. Place in pan. Drizzle with oil; sprinkle with salt. Toss to coat; spread squash in single layer.

3 Bake 8 to 10 minutes or just until tender.

1 Serving: Calories 40; Total Fat 2.5g (Saturated Fat 0g, Trans Fat 0g); Cholesterol 0mg; Sodium 150mg; Total Carbohydrate 3g (Dietary Fiber 1g); Protein 1g **Exchanges:** ½ Vegetable, ½ Fat **Carbohydrate Choices:** 0

> FRESH FACT Straight, even vegetables work best when using a spiralizer. If you don't have a spiralizer, use a vegetable peeler. Pull peeler down sides of squash, making long strips. The baking time may be less.

Prep Time:
25 Minutes

Start to Finish:
25 Minutes

4 servings

Kohlrabi might not currently be in your repertoire, but give this mild vegetable a try. Here it is cooked to caramelized perfection and topped with fresh herbs and goat cheese.

Caramelized Kohlrabi with Goat Cheese

4	medium kohlrabi (1 to 1¼ lb)	¼	teaspoon coarse ground black pepper
1	tablespoon olive oil	¼	cup softened chèvre (goat) cheese (1 oz)
1	tablespoon butter	1	tablespoon chopped fresh chives
¼	teaspoon salt	1	teaspoon grated lemon peel

1 Cut stems and ends off kohlrabi; carefully peel. Cut in half; remove core. Place kohlrabi, cut sides down, on cutting board; cut into ¼-inch slices.

2 In 12-inch skillet, heat oil and butter over medium heat until butter is melted. Arrange kohlrabi slices in single layer in skillet, overlapping slightly if necessary; sprinkle with salt and pepper. Cook 6 to 8 minutes, turning once, until tender and golden brown. (Cook in two batches to get more caramelization.)

3 Place slices on warm serving platter. Top with dollops of cheese; sprinkle with chives and lemon peel.

1 Serving: Calories 150; Total Fat 11g (Saturated Fat 6g, Trans Fat 0g); Cholesterol 20mg; Sodium 280mg; Total Carbohydrate 7g (Dietary Fiber 4g); Protein 6g **Exchanges:** 1½ Vegetable, ½ Medium-Fat Meat, 1½ Fat **Carbohydrate Choices:** ½

> FRESH FACT Kohlrabi, also called cabbage turnip, is a member of the turnip family. The pale green or purple-white bulb tastes similar to a sweet, mild turnip. Both the bulb and greens are edible. The smallest bulbs are the most tender. Purchase kohlrabi that is firm, heavy and unblemished. Turnips can also be substituted.

> TRY THIS If you're not a fan of goat cheese, substitute mascarpone or cream cheese.

Stir-fry sauce and sesame seed give green beans an Asian flair in a quick-to-make skillet side.

Prep Time:
15 Minutes

Start to Finish:
15 Minutes

6 servings

Spicy Stir-Fried Green Beans

⅓ cup stir-fry sauce

2 teaspoons chili garlic paste

2 tablespoons vegetable oil

6 cups fresh green beans, trimmed

1 teaspoon sesame seed

1 In medium bowl, mix stir-fry sauce and chili garlic paste; set aside.

2 In 12-inch nonstick skillet, heat oil over medium-high heat. Toss green beans in oil; cook 5 to 7 minutes, stirring every minute, until bright green and crisp-tender. (Mixture may splatter during cooking.* Beans will sizzle, blister and brown in spots.)

3 With slotted spoon, remove beans from skillet; add to sauce mixture in bowl. Toss to coat. Transfer to serving bowl; sprinkle with sesame seed.

*Use a splatter guard screen, available at many department and specialty food stores, for recipes like this that tend to splatter during cooking.

1 Serving: Calories 100; Total Fat 5g (Saturated Fat 1g, Trans Fat 0g); Cholesterol 0mg; Sodium 470mg; Total Carbohydrate 11g (Dietary Fiber 4g); Protein 2g **Exchanges:** ½ Other Carbohydrate, 1 Vegetable, 1 Fat **Carbohydrate Choices:** 1

You can purchase peeled, seeded and cubed butternut squash from many grocery stores. This prepared fresh food is perfect for recipes like this one that come together in minutes after the squash is prepared.

Prep Time:
15 Minutes

Start to Finish:
25 Minutes

6 servings
(½ cup each)

Asian Butternut Squash

¼ cup water	2 tablespoons soy sauce
1 small butternut squash, peeled, seeded, cut into ½-inch pieces (about 4 cups)	1½ teaspoons chili oil
	¼ cup chopped green onions (4 medium)
3 tablespoons packed brown sugar	

1 In 10-inch nonstick skillet, heat water to boiling. Add squash; reduce heat to medium. Cover; simmer 7 to 10 minutes or until squash is almost tender when pierced with fork.

2 In small bowl, mix brown sugar, soy sauce and chili oil. Stir soy sauce mixture into squash and water in skillet. Heat to boiling; reduce heat to medium-low. Cook uncovered 2 minutes, stirring occasionally. Stir in onions; cook 2 minutes longer, stirring frequently, until squash is tender.

1 Serving: Calories 80; Total Fat 1g (Saturated Fat 0g, Trans Fat 0g); Cholesterol 0mg; Sodium 310mg; Total Carbohydrate 16g (Dietary Fiber 1g); Protein 1g **Exchanges:** 1 Other Carbohydrate, ½ Vegetable **Carbohydrate Choices:** 1

> FRESH FACT Chili oil is vegetable oil that has been infused with chili peppers. Characteristically red in color, it adds spicy heat to Asian dishes. Look for it near other Asian products at your supermarket. Once opened, it can be stored up to 6 months at room temperature, or longer if refrigerated.

Warm and homey spices in a flavorful glaze elevate baby carrots from a grab-and-go snack to a sophisticated side. Your microwave makes preparation a snap.

Prep Time:
20 Minutes

Start to Finish:
20 Minutes

6 servings
(½ cup each)

Gingered Baby Carrots

1   **bag (16 oz) ready-to-eat baby-cut carrots**

¼   **cup chopped pecans**

3   **tablespoons packed brown sugar**

⅛   **teaspoon ground cinnamon**

1   **tablespoon butter**

1   **tablespoon honey**

1   **tablespoon finely chopped gingerroot**

1 In 1-quart microwavable casserole, place carrots and 2 tablespoons water; cover. Microwave on High 7 to 10 minutes until crisp-tender. Let stand covered 5 minutes.

2 Meanwhile, in 8-inch skillet, cook pecans, 1 tablespoon of the brown sugar and the cinnamon over medium heat about 3 minutes, stirring frequently, until pecans are toasted and glazed. Remove from skillet to small bowl; set aside.

3 In same skillet, cook remaining 2 tablespoons brown sugar, the butter, honey and gingerroot over medium heat, stirring constantly, until bubbly.

4 Drain carrots; add to skillet. Cook 2 to 3 minutes, stirring frequently, until carrots are glazed and hot. Sprinkle with pecans.

1 Serving: Calories 160; Total Fat 9g (Saturated Fat 2g, Trans Fat 0g); Cholesterol 5mg; Sodium 70mg; Total Carbohydrate 18g (Dietary Fiber 3g); Protein 1g **Exchanges:** 1 Other Carbohydrate, 1 Vegetable, 2 Fat **Carbohydrate Choices:** 1

> TRY THIS Instead of baby carrots, you can substitute whole carrots. Peel the carrots and cut them into ¾-inch slices.

Edamame and bacon make for a hearty side or a light meal.

Prep Time:
25 Minutes

Start to Finish:
25 Minutes

7 servings
(½ cup each)

Edamame-Corn Toss

2 slices thick-sliced bacon, cut crosswise in half

½ cup chopped red bell pepper

1½ cups frozen shelled edamame (green soybeans), thawed

2½ cups frozen whole kernel corn, thawed

½ cup half-and-half

2 tablespoons chopped fresh oregano leaves

¼ teaspoon salt

¼ teaspoon pepper

1 In 2-quart saucepan, cook bacon over medium-high heat until crisp. Drain on paper towels. Crumble bacon; set aside. Reserve 1 tablespoon drippings in saucepan.

2 Cook bell pepper in bacon drippings over medium heat 2 to 3 minutes, stirring occasionally, until tender. Add edamame and corn; cook 3 minutes, stirring occasionally. Stir in half-and-half, oregano, salt and pepper.

3 Cover; cook 5 to 6 minutes longer, stirring occasionally, until vegetables are tender. Stir in bacon.

1 Serving: Calories 140; Total Fat 6g (Saturated Fat 2g, Trans Fat 0g); Cholesterol 10mg; Sodium 170mg; Total Carbohydrate 16g (Dietary Fiber 3g); Protein 7g **Exchanges:** ½ Starch, 1 Vegetable, ½ Very Lean Meat, 1 Fat **Carbohydrate Choices:** 1

Prep Time:
25 Minutes

Start to Finish:
25 Minutes

6 servings

Brussels sprouts have gotten a bad rap over the years as tasting more like medicine than delicious food. Nothing could be further from the truth. Cooked in bacon drippings and served with cranberries, bacon and pistachios, this versatile vegetable really shines.

Cranberry-Pistachio Brussels Sprouts

2	slices thick-sliced bacon	⅓	cup sweetened dried cranberries
1	lb Brussels sprouts, trimmed, cut in half	¼	cup salted roasted pistachio nuts
¼	cup chicken broth	1	tablespoon honey
		¼	teaspoon cracked black pepper

1 In 10-inch skillet, cook bacon over medium-high heat until crisp. Drain on paper towels. Crumble bacon; set aside. Reserve 1 tablespoon drippings in skillet.

2 Cook Brussels sprouts in bacon drippings over medium heat 3 to 4 minutes, stirring frequently, until they just begin to brown. Add broth; reduce heat to medium-low. Cover; cook 5 to 6 minutes longer or until broth is evaporated and Brussels sprouts are tender.

3 Add cranberries, nuts, honey, pepper and bacon; toss to coat.

1 Serving: Calories 110; Total Fat 4.5g (Saturated Fat 1g, Trans Fat 0g); Cholesterol 0mg; Sodium 170mg; Total Carbohydrate 14g (Dietary Fiber 2g); Protein 4g **Exchanges:** ½ Starch, 1 Vegetable, 1 Fat **Carbohydrate Choices:** 1

Cauliflower has recently emerged as a culinary hero because of its versatility, and this recipe makes the most of its texture, flavor and ability to work well with diverse ingredients.

Prep Time:
25 Minutes

Start to Finish:
25 Minutes

4 servings
(¾ cup each)

Sautéed Cauliflower with Browned Bread Crumbs

1	medium head cauliflower (2 lb), separated into florets	2	cups soft bread crumbs (about 3 slices bread)
4	tablespoons butter	2	tablespoons olive oil
1	tablespoon Dijon mustard		

1 In 10-inch skillet, heat 1 inch water (salted, if desired) to boiling. Add cauliflower; return to boiling. Boil uncovered 3 minutes or until almost tender; drain. Immediately rinse under cold water to stop cooking; set aside.

2 In same skillet, melt 3 tablespoons of the butter over medium heat. Stir mustard into butter; add bread crumbs. Cook 8 to 10 minutes, stirring frequently, until crumbs are golden brown. Remove crumbs to plate.

3 Wipe out skillet with paper towel. Add remaining 1 tablespoon butter and the oil; heat over medium-high heat. Stir in cauliflower. Cook about 5 minutes, stirring occasionally, until lightly browned and tender. Sprinkle crumbs over top.

1 Serving: Calories 420; Total Fat 22g (Saturated Fat 7g, Trans Fat 0.5g); Cholesterol 30mg; Sodium 1270mg; Total Carbohydrate 47g (Dietary Fiber 5g); Protein 10g **Exchanges:** 2½ Starch, ½ Other Carbohydrate, 1 Vegetable, 4 Fat **Carbohydrate Choices:** 3

Frozen vegetables, which retain so many of the nutrients when picked, are the stars of the show in a savory side dish that your family will love.

Prep Time:
20 Minutes

Start to Finish:
20 Minutes

6 servings
(½ cup each)

Peas and Corn with Thyme Butter

3	slices bacon, cut into ½-inch pieces	2	tablespoons water
2	cups frozen baby sweet peas	¼	to ½ teaspoon dried thyme leaves
2	cups frozen whole kernel corn	2	tablespoons butter

1 In 12-inch nonstick skillet, cook bacon over medium heat, stirring frequently, until crisp. Remove bacon with slotted spoon; drain on paper towels. Reserve 1 tablespoon drippings in skillet.

2 Add peas, corn and water to bacon drippings. Cover; cook over medium heat 6 to 8 minutes, stirring occasionally, until vegetables are tender and water has evaporated.

3 Stir in thyme and butter until vegetables are coated. Sprinkle with bacon.

1 Serving: Calories 160; Total Fat 8g (Saturated Fat 3.5g, Trans Fat 0g); Cholesterol 15mg; Sodium 220mg; Total Carbohydrate 16g (Dietary Fiber 3g); Protein 5g **Exchanges:** 1 Starch, 1½ Fat **Carbohydrate Choices:** 1

This clever side dish combines the creamy, comforting texture of smashed potatoes with the flavors of Mexican favorites for a creative side dish you'll love.

Prep Time:
10 Minutes

Start to Finish:
30 Minutes

6 servings
(½ cup each)

Smashed Mexican Potatoes

1   lb small red potatoes, cut into 1-inch pieces

½   cup black beans (from 15-oz can), drained, rinsed

½   cup frozen whole kernel corn

½   cup shredded Colby-Monterey Jack cheese blend (2 oz)

2   tablespoons chopped fresh cilantro

½   teaspoon ground cumin

½   teaspoon salt

1   to 2 tablespoons milk

1 In 2-quart saucepan, place potatoes and enough water to cover. Heat to boiling; reduce heat. Cover; simmer 14 to 18 minutes or until potatoes are tender when pierced with fork. Drain.

2 Return potatoes to saucepan; shake saucepan gently over low heat 1 to 2 minutes to evaporate any excess moisture. Remove from heat. Mash potatoes with fork or potato masher, leaving some potato pieces in chunks. Cover to keep warm.

3 In small microwavable bowl, stir together beans and corn; cover. Microwave on High 2 to 3 minutes or until hot.

4 Gently fold bean mixture, cheese, cilantro, cumin and salt into mashed potatoes. Stir in milk, 1 tablespoon at a time, until desired consistency.

1 Serving: Calories 130; Total Fat 3.5g (Saturated Fat 2g, Trans Fat 0g); Cholesterol 10mg; Sodium 310mg; Total Carbohydrate 20g (Dietary Fiber 3g); Protein 5g **Exchanges:** 1 Starch, ½ Vegetable, ½ Fat **Carbohydrate Choices:** 1

> TRY THIS For even more Mexican flavor, garnish the potatoes with sliced avocado and a dollop of sour cream.

The colorful vegetables in this dish look stunning in the hash browns, and fresh herbs amp up the flavor for a side dish you'll make again and again.

Prep Time:
25 Minutes

Start to Finish:
25 Minutes

4 servings
(½ cup each)

Herbed Confetti Hash Browns

2   tablespoons olive oil

2   cups refrigerated cooked diced potatoes with onions (from 20-oz bag)

1   medium carrot, chopped

1   medium zucchini, chopped

1   teaspoon chopped fresh rosemary leaves

1   teaspoon chopped fresh thyme leaves

¾   teaspoon salt

½   teaspoon garlic powder

1   In 12-inch nonstick skillet, heat oil over medium heat. Stir in remaining ingredients. Cook 15 to 20 minutes, stirring occasionally, until potatoes are golden brown and vegetables are tender.

1 Serving: Calories 140; Total Fat 7g (Saturated Fat 1g, Trans Fat 0g); Cholesterol 0mg; Sodium 590mg; Total Carbohydrate 17g (Dietary Fiber 2g); Protein 2g **Exchanges:** 1 Other Carbohydrate, 1 Vegetable, 1½ Fat **Carbohydrate Choices:** 1

Prep Time: 15 Minutes • Start to Finish: 1 Hour 15 Minutes • 3 1/2 cups

Fresh Salsa

- 3 large tomatoes, seeded, chopped (3 cups)
- 1 small green bell pepper, chopped (½ cup)
- 8 medium green onions, sliced (½ cup)
- 3 cloves garlic, finely chopped
- 2 tablespoons chopped fresh cilantro
- 1 tablespoon finely chopped seeded jalapeño chiles
- 2 to 3 tablespoons lime juice
- ½ teaspoon salt

1 In medium glass or plastic bowl, mix all ingredients. Cover and refrigerate at least 1 hour to blend flavors. Store covered refrigerator up to 1 week.

Black bean salsa: Stir in 1 can (15 oz) black beans, drained and rinsed. Makes about 5 cups.

¼ cup: Calories 15; Total Fat 0g (Saturated Fat 0g, Trans Fat 0g); Cholesterol 0mg; Sodium 90mg; Total Carbohydrate 3g (Dietary Fiber 0g); Protein 0g **Exchanges:** Free **Carbohydrate Choices**: 0

> GO-WITH IDEA The fresh flavor of this salsa will have you using it with everything! It makes a great topping for omelets or scrambled eggs, a simple appetizer when spooned over a block of cream cheese to serve with crackers or mixed with sour cream for a yummy dip.

Prep Time: 15 Minutes • Start to Finish: 24 Hours 15 Minutes • 6 cups

Spicy Pickled Vegetables

- 3 cups white wine vinegar
- 1½ cups sugar
- 2 cloves garlic, finely chopped
- 1 medium head cauliflower (1½ lb), separated into small florets (6 cups)
- ½ lb fresh green beans, trimmed
- 2 medium carrots, cut into 3x¼x¼-inch pieces (1½ cups)
- 2 jalapeño chiles, cut lengthwise into quarters, seeded

1 In 1-quart saucepan, heat vinegar, sugar and garlic over medium heat just until mixture begins to simmer and sugar is dissolved. Remove from heat; cool 5 minutes.

2 Meanwhile, in 2 (1-quart) jars or glass containers, layer cauliflower, beans, carrots and chiles, dividing evenly between jars. Pour vinegar mixture over vegetables. Cover; refrigerate at least 24 hours before serving. Store covered in refrigerator up to 2 weeks.

¼ Cup: Calories 70; Total Fat 0g (Saturated Fat 0g, Trans Fat 0g); Cholesterol 0mg; Sodium 15mg; Total Carbohydrate 16g (Dietary Fiber 1g); Protein 1g **Exchanges:** 1 Other Carbohydrate, ½ Vegetable **Carbohydrate Choices:** 1

Prep Time: 15 Minutes • Start to Finish: 24 Hours 15 Minutes • 6 cups

Easy Refrigerator Pickles

6	cups thinly sliced unpeeled unwaxed cucumbers
2	small onions, sliced
1	medium carrot, thinly sliced (½ cup)
1¾	cups sugar
2	tablespoons salt
1	tablespoon chopped fresh or 1 teaspoon dried dill weed
1	cup white or cider vinegar

1 In 2½- or 3-quart glass container, layer cucumbers, onions and carrot.

2 In medium bowl, stir together remaining ingredients until sugar is dissolved; pour over vegetables. Cover; refrigerate at least 24 hours before serving. Store covered in refrigerator up to 2 weeks.

¼ Cup: Calories 70; Total Fat 0g (Saturated Fat 0g, Trans Fat 0g); Cholesterol 0mg; Sodium 590mg; Total Carbohydrate 16g (Dietary Fiber 0g); Protein 0g **Exchanges:** 1 Other Carbohydrate **Carbohydrate Choices:** 1

> FRESH FACT When choosing cucumbers for pickles, pick out the smaller ones and pickle them soon after buying or harvesting. Use unwaxed cucumbers for pickles as the pickling solution does not penetrate the wax coating.

Prep Time: 15 Minutes • Start to Finish: 24 Hours 15 Minutes • 6 cups

Crunchy Veggie Relish

6	cups finely chopped green cabbage
2	medium cucumbers, peeled, shredded (3 cups)
1	medium red bell pepper, chopped (1 cup)
1	cup sugar
1½	teaspoons salt
1	teaspoon mustard seed
½	teaspoon celery seed
½	cup white or cider vinegar

1 In large bowl, mix all ingredients. Spoon into 1-quart and 1-pint jars or plastic containers.

2 Cover; refrigerate at least 24 hours before serving. Store covered in refrigerator up to 2 weeks.

¼ Cup: Calories 45; Total Fat 0g (Saturated Fat 0g, Trans Fat 0g); Cholesterol 0mg; Sodium 150mg; Total Carbohydrate 10g (Dietary Fiber 0g); Protein 0g **Exchanges:** ½ Other Carbohydrate, 1 Vegetable **Carbohydrate Choices:** ½

Prep Time: **10 Minutes** • Start to Finish: **24 Hours 10 Minutes** • **3½ cups**

Prep Time: **10 Minutes** • Start to Finish: **24 Hours 20 Minutes** • **5 half-pints**

Pickled Tarragon Baby Carrots

Strawberry Freezer Jam

1	bag (16 oz) ready-to-eat baby-cut carrots
½	cup tarragon vinegar
1	tablespoon chopped fresh or 1 teaspoon dried tarragon leaves
1	tablespoon olive or vegetable oil
¼	teaspoon coarse ground black pepper

1	quart (4 cups) strawberries, cut in half
4	cups sugar
¾	cup water
1	package (1¾ oz) powdered fruit pectin

1 In 3-quart saucepan, heat 2 quarts water to boiling. Add carrots; cook 3 minutes.

2 Meanwhile, in 1- to 1½-quart heatproof glass or plastic container, mix remaining ingredients. Drain carrots; immediately stir into mixture in container.

3 Cover; refrigerate 24 hours, stirring once, before serving. Store covered in refrigerator up to 3 months.

¼ Cup: Calories 25; Total Fat 1g (Saturated Fat 0g, Trans Fat 0g); Cholesterol 0mg; Sodium 25mg; Total Carbohydrate 3g (Dietary Fiber 1g); Protein 0g **Exchanges:** ½ Vegetable **Carbohydrate Choices:** 0

1 In large bowl, mash strawberries with potato masher to make 2 cups crushed strawberries. Add sugar; mix well. Let stand at room temperature 10 minutes, stirring occasionally.

2 In 1-quart saucepan, mix water and pectin until pectin is dissolved. Heat to a full rolling boil that cannot be stirred down, stirring constantly. Boil hard 1 minute, continuing to stir. Pour hot pectin mixture over strawberry mixture; stir constantly until sugar is completely dissolved, about 3 minutes.

3 Immediately pour mixture into freezer containers, leaving ½-inch headspace; cover. Let stand at room temperature 24 hours or until set.

4 Store in freezer up to 12 months or in refrigerator up to 3 weeks. Thaw in refrigerator before serving.

1 Tablespoon: Calories 45; Total Fat 0g (Saturated Fat 0g, Trans Fat 0g); Cholesterol 0mg; Sodium 0mg; Total Carbohydrate 11g (Dietary Fiber 0g); Protein 0g **Exchanges:** ½ Other Carbohydrate **Carbohydrate Choices:** 1

Prep Time: 10 Minutes • Start to Finish: 24 Hours 20 Minutes • 6 half-pints

Berry Pomegranate Jam

- **2** cups each strawberries, cut in half, and raspberries
- **1** cup blueberries
- **4¼** cups sugar
- **¾** cup pomegranate juice
- **1** package (1¾ oz) powdered fruit pectin

1 In large bowl, mash berries with potato masher to make 2½ cups crushed berries. Add sugar; mix well. Let stand at room temperature 10 minutes, stirring occasionally.

2 In 1-quart saucepan, mix juice and pectin until pectin is dissolved. Heat to a full rolling boil that cannot be stirred down, stirring constantly. Boil hard 1 minute, continuing to stir. Pour hot pectin mixture over berry mixture; stir constantly until sugar is completely dissolved, about 3 minutes.

3 Immediately pour mixture into hot sterilized jars or freezer containers, leaving ½-inch headspace; cover. Let stand at room temperature about 24 hours or until set.

4 Store in freezer up to 12 months or in refrigerator up to 3 weeks. Thaw frozen jam in refrigerator and stir before serving.

1 Tablespoon: Calories 40; Total Fat 0g (Saturated Fat 0g, Trans Fat 0g); Cholesterol 0mg; Sodium 0mg; Total Carbohydrate 10g (Dietary Fiber 0g); Protein 0g **Exchanges:** ½ Other Carbohydrate **Carbohydrate Choices:** ½

Prep Time: 10 Minutes • Start to Finish: 2 Hours 10 Minutes • 1 cup

Spiced Apricot Ginger Preserves

- **1** cup apricot or peach preserves
- **1** tablespoon finely chopped crystallized ginger
- **1** tablespoon orange-flavored liqueur or orange juice
- **¼** teaspoon ground nutmeg

1 In 1-quart saucepan, mix all ingredients. Heat to boiling; boil 1 minute, stirring frequently. Remove from heat; cool 2 hours.

2 Spoon into glass or plastic container. Store covered in refrigerator up to 2 months.

1 Tablespoon: Calories 60; Total Fat 0g (Saturated Fat 0g, Trans Fat 0g); Cholesterol 0mg; Sodium 5mg; Total Carbohydrate 15g (Dietary Fiber 0g); Protein 0g **Exchanges:** 1 Other Carbohydrate **Carbohydrate Choices:** 1

CHAPTER 6

Fruit Desserts

A fun and quick dessert for after dinner, or a perfect treat for the dessert table at your next buffet. Fresh berries add a homey touch.

Prep Time:
20 Minutes

Start to Finish:
20 Minutes

8 servings

Chocolate Berry Shooters

⅔ cup whipping cream

1 cup semisweet or dark chocolate chips

1 teaspoon vanilla

1 cup coarsely chopped fresh strawberries

24 fresh raspberries

Sweetened whipped cream, if desired

Additional strawberries and raspberries, if desired

1 In medium microwavable bowl, microwave whipping cream uncovered on High 45 seconds to 1 minute or just until it begins to boil. Stir in chocolate chips and vanilla with whisk until chips are melted and smooth. Let stand 5 minutes.

2 Meanwhile, spoon about 2 tablespoons strawberries in bottom of each of 8 (3-oz) shot glasses or other small glasses; top each with 3 raspberries. Carefully spoon chocolate mixture evenly over berries.

3 For a soft and smooth dessert, serve immediately. Or freeze 15 minutes to firm up (mixture will be similar to ganache). Garnish with whipped cream and additional berries.

1 Serving: Calories 200; Total Fat 14g (Saturated Fat 8g, Trans Fat 0g); Cholesterol 25mg; Sodium 10mg; Total Carbohydrate 16g (Dietary Fiber 2g); Protein 1g **Exchanges:** 1 Other Carbohydrate, 3 Fat **Carbohydrate Choices:** 1

> TRY THIS These shooters can be made a day ahead of serving. After spooning chocolate over berries, refrigerate uncovered about 20 minutes or until set. Then cover and refrigerate until serving time.

> FRESH FACT Myth buster! Yes, you can freeze sweetened whipped cream. To have dollops ready at any time, line a cookie sheet with waxed paper or foil. Drop whipped cream by spoonfuls onto cookie sheet. Freeze uncovered at least 2 hours. Place frozen mounds of whipped cream in freezer container; cover tightly. Freeze up to 2 months.

Prep Time:
15 Minutes

Start to Finish:
15 Minutes

4 servings

Açai was hailed as a superfood when it first became popular. It contains antioxidants and heart-healthy fats, but more importantly, it's delicious! Açai berry juice is an easy way to add this South American native to your diet, and this frozen, fruity dessert is a wonderful way to enjoy açai.

Açai Berry Lava Flows

1	**bag (10 oz) frozen unsweetened strawberries**
¾	**cup açai berry juice**
½	**cup light rum**
¼	**cup sugar**
8	**ice cubes**

1	**cup vanilla fat-free frozen yogurt**
2	**tablespoons canned cream of coconut (not coconut milk)**
⅔	**cup cold water**
4	**fresh strawberries, if desired**
4	**sprigs fresh mint, if desired**

1 In blender, place frozen strawberries, juice, rum and sugar. Cover; blend on high speed about 1 minute 30 seconds or until smooth. Pour evenly into 4 (8-oz) wine or other stemmed glasses (about ½ cup each). Rinse blender.

2 Add ice cubes to blender. Cover; blend on high speed until crushed. Add frozen yogurt, cream of coconut and water. Cover; blend on high speed about 1 minute 30 seconds or until smooth. Spoon evenly on top of strawberry mixture in glasses (generous ⅓ cup each). Garnish with fresh strawberries and mint. Serve immediately.

1 Serving: Calories 240; Total Fat 3g (Saturated Fat 2.5g, Trans Fat 0g); Cholesterol 0mg; Sodium 50mg; Total Carbohydrate 35g (Dietary Fiber 2g); Protein 2g **Carbohydrate Choices:** 2

> TRY THIS If you prefer not to use rum, add an extra ¼ cup açai berry juice instead.

Yum! This South-of-the-Border ice cream is bursting with fresh fruit flavor and fresh blueberries.

Prep Time:
10 Minutes

Start to Finish:
30 Minutes

16 servings

Blueberry Margarita Ice Cream

2 **cups cold whipping cream**	2 **tablespoons cold tequila**
1 **cup cold whole milk**	2 **tablespoons cold fresh lime juice**
1 **cup powdered sugar**	2 **cups chilled fresh blueberries**
3 **tablespoons cold orange-flavored liqueur**	

1 In large bowl, mix whipping cream, milk, ½ cup of the powdered sugar, the liqueur, tequila and lime juice with whisk until well blended.

2 In medium bowl, mash blueberries and remaining ½ cup powdered sugar with pastry blender or potato masher, or process in food processor until slightly chunky (not pureed); stir into cream mixture.

3 Pour into 1-quart ice-cream freezer and freeze according to manufacturer's directions.* Eat immediately for soft-serve ice cream. Or remove from freezer cylinder and place in freezer container; cover tightly and freeze until firm.

*This recipe was tested using an electric ice-cream maker with a frozen cylinder insert. Most of these models make ice cream in about 25 minutes. Ours was ready in 18 minutes. Make sure all ingredients are cold before starting, as indicated in the recipe; this will help the mixture freeze faster.

1 Serving: Calories 170; Total Fat 12g (Saturated Fat 7g, Trans Fat 0g); Cholesterol 40mg; Sodium 20mg; Total Carbohydrate 13g (Dietary Fiber 0g); Protein 1g **Carbohydrate Choices:** 1

15 MINUTES OR LESS

Fresh strawberries and mango pair beautifully with caramel sauce in this quick but elegant dessert.

Prep Time:
15 Minutes

Start to Finish:
15 Minutes

15 servings

Dulce de Leche Fillo Cups

2 oz ⅓-less-fat cream cheese (Neufchâtel), softened

2 tablespoons dulce de leche (caramel) syrup

1 tablespoon reduced-fat sour cream

1 package (1.9 oz) frozen mini fillo (phyllo) shells (15 shells)

⅓ cup sliced fresh strawberries

2 tablespoons diced mango

1 In small bowl, beat cream cheese with electric mixer on low speed until creamy. Beat in syrup and sour cream until blended.

2 Spoon cream cheese mixture into each fillo shell. Top with strawberries and mango.

1 Serving: Calories 40; Total Fat 2g (Saturated Fat 0.5g, Trans Fat 0g); Cholesterol 0mg; Sodium 35mg; Total Carbohydrate 4g (Dietary Fiber 0g); Protein 0g **Exchanges:** ½ Other Carbohydrate, ½ Fat **Carbohydrate Choices:** 0

Pineapple

Tropical, fragrant and with a sweet-tangy flavor, pineapple is a wonderful fruit to eat fresh or use in a variety of recipes. Purchase pineapple that has a fresh, sweet aroma. The fruit should be firm and not have any soft spots or wrinkled skin. The pineapple leaves should be firm and fresh-looking.

Store whole fresh pineapple at room temperature for 1 to 2 days, and then refrigerate. To cut a pineapple, use a sharp knife and start by cutting off the green leaves and about ½ inch from the top of the pineapple. Stand the pineapple upright and cut away the skin from top to bottom, following the shape of the fruit. If you don't remove all of the "eyes," you can do it after with a melon baller or the tip of a vegetable peeler. Then cut the pineapple into slices; remove the center of each slice with a sharp knife. Store cut pineapple in the refrigerator for up to 5 days.

Here are some delicious ways to use pineapple.

PINEAPPLE SALSA In medium bowl, mix 1 cup chopped fresh pineapple, ½ cup chopped red bell pepper, ¼ cup chopped green onion, 2 tablespoons chopped fresh cilantro, 1 small finely chopped jalapeno chile, 2 tablespoons lime juice and 1 tablespoon honey. Serve over everything from grilled fish to baked chicken, or use as a delicious dip for corn chips.

HAM AND PINEAPPLE KABOBS Alternately thread ham cubes, pineapple wedges and cherry tomatoes onto metal skewers. In small bowl, combine ¼ cup red currant jelly and 1 tablespoon mustard; microwave on High for 1 to 2 minutes, stirring every 30 seconds. Brush over kabobs and grill over medium heat for 4 to 6 minutes or until glazed, turning once.

FROZEN PINEAPPLE POPS Insert wooden skewers into 3x1-inch pieces of pineapple. Dip pineapple into ½ cup orange juice and roll in ¾ cup shredded coconut. Cover and freeze 1 to 2 hours.

PINEAPPLE-CHICKEN SALAD In large bowl, toss 1 cup each baby spinach and torn romaine. Top with small pineapple wedges, chopped cooked chicken and diced bell pepper. In small bowl, stir ⅓ cup Italian dressing and 3 tablespoons orange marmalade. Drizzle dressing over salad. Sprinkle with cashews.

PINEAPPLE OATMEAL Make steel-cut or old-fashioned oatmeal as directed on the package. Top each serving with ¼ cup pineapple wedges and 1 to 2 tablespoons maple syrup.

PINEAPPLE-CARROT SLAW In medium bowl, toss 1 cup julienne-cut carrots, 1 cup diced pineapple, ¼ cup chopped green onions, 2 tablespoons lime juice, 1 tablespoon vegetable oil, 2 tablespoons chopped fresh cilantro and ½ cup chopped honey-roasted peanuts..

Grilling pineapple brings out its natural sweetness and softens the fruit. A creamy topping really takes this dessert over the edge!

Prep Time:
30 Minutes

Start to Finish:
30 Minutes

6 servings

Grilled Pineapple Slices with Ginger Cream

½   **cup plain fat-free yogurt or fat-free sour cream**

1   **tablespoon packed brown sugar**

1   **tablespoon chopped crystallized ginger**

1   **medium pineapple (3 lb)**

1   **tablespoon butter, melted**

6   **maraschino cherries**

1   Heat gas or charcoal grill. In small bowl, mix yogurt, brown sugar and ginger. Cover; refrigerate until serving time.

2   Cut ½-inch slice off top and bottom of pineapple. Cut off rind. Cut pineapple crosswise into 6 slices; remove "eyes" from slices. Drizzle both sides of pineapple slices with melted butter.

3   Place pineapple slices on grill over medium heat. Cover grill; cook 10 to 15 minutes, turning once, until hot and light brown.

4   To serve, top pineapple with ginger cream; garnish with cherries.

1 Serving: Calories 120; Total Fat 2g (Saturated Fat 0g, Trans Fat 0.5g); Cholesterol 0mg; Sodium 55mg; Total Carbohydrate 24g (Dietary Fiber 2g); Protein 1g **Exchanges:** 1 Fruit, ½ Other Carbohydrate, ½ Fat **Carbohydrate Choices:** 1½

> TRY THIS Grilled pineapple is also delicious with fresh whipped cream, ice cream, yogurt, sorbet or sherbet.

15 MINUTES OR LESS

Everyone will love this grown-up fruit cocktail with fresh fruit and champagne. If you're making it for kids, swap out the champagne for sparkling white grape juice, which is also delicious.

Mimosa Fruit Cups

¼ **cup sugar**	1 **large pear, cut into bite-size pieces**
1 **teaspoon grated orange peel**	1 **cup seedless green grapes**
1 **cup fresh orange juice**	1 **large banana, sliced**
1 **large orange, peeled, cut into bite-size pieces**	1½ **cups champagne or sparkling white grape juice**
1 **large red apple, cut into bite-size pieces**	**Fresh mint sprigs, if desired**

1 In large bowl, stir sugar, orange peel and orange juice until sugar is dissolved. Gently stir in orange, apple, pear and grapes until coated.

2 Stir in banana and champagne. Spoon about ¾ cup fruit with juice into each of 8 footed dessert cups. Garnish with mint.

1 Serving: Calories 130; Total Fat 0g (Saturated Fat 0g, Trans Fat 0g); Cholesterol 0mg; Sodium 0mg; Total Carbohydrate 28g (Dietary Fiber 3g); Protein 1g **Exchanges:** ½ Starch, ½ Fruit, 1 Other Carbohydrate **Carbohydrate Choices:** 2

> TRY THIS The recipe can be prepared through Step 1, then covered and refrigerated at least 1 hour or overnight. Stir in banana and champagne just before serving.

A fun and fruity idea for your next party, this coconut- and rum-infused dip works beautifully with any kind of fruit, but pairs especially well with more tropical fruits like pineapple and kiwi.

Prep Time:
25 Minutes

Start to Finish:
25 Minutes

15 servings

Fruit with Piña Colada Dip

2	containers (6 oz each) vanilla fat-free yogurt
1	teaspoon rum extract or dark rum
3	tablespoons flaked coconut, toasted*
2	tablespoons finely chopped pineapple

15	fresh strawberries, cut in half
30	chunks (1 inch) fresh pineapple
30	chunks peeled kiwifruit (about 5 medium)

> **TIME-SAVER** The dip can be made up to 1 day in advance— except wait to sprinkle with the remaining toasted coconut; cover and refrigerate. Before serving, stir the dip and then top with coconut.

1 In small bowl, stir together yogurt, rum extract and 2 tablespoons of the coconut until well blended. Stir in chopped pineapple. Sprinkle with remaining 1 tablespoon coconut.

2 Place bowl of dip on serving platter. Arrange strawberries, pineapple chunks and kiwifruit around bowl.

*To toast coconut, sprinkle in ungreased skillet. Cook over medium-low heat 6 to 14 minutes, stirring frequently until browning begins, then stirring constantly until golden brown.

1 Serving: Calories 60; Total Fat 0.5g (Saturated Fat 0g, Trans Fat 0g); Cholesterol 0mg; Sodium 15mg; Total Carbohydrate 11g (Dietary Fiber 1g); Protein 1g **Exchanges:** 1 Fruit **Carbohydrate Choices:** 1

Ice cream becomes a fresh treat when paired with cantaloupe and topped with nuts.

Butter Pecan Cantaloupe Wedges

1	large cantaloupe	1	cup real maple syrup
1	pint (2 cups) butter pecan ice cream	8	pecan halves

Prep Time:
10 Minutes

Start to Finish:
10 Minutes

8 servings

1 Cut cantaloupe in half; remove seeds. Cut each half into 8 wedges. Remove peel from each wedge.

2 For each serving, arrange 2 cantaloupe wedges in shallow bowl. Top with ¼ cup ice cream. Drizzle with 2 tablespoons syrup. Top with pecan half. Serve immediately.

1 Serving: Calories 220; Total Fat 5g (Saturated Fat 2.5g, Trans Fat 0g); Cholesterol 15mg; Sodium 45mg; Total Carbohydrate 43g (Dietary Fiber 1g); Protein 2g **Exchanges:** ½ Fruit, 2½ Other Carbohydrate, 1 Fat **Carbohydrate Choices:** 3

Prep Time:
10 Minutes

Start to Finish:
10 Minutes

4 servings

Everyone loves parfaits, and they will especially love these berry-filled yogurt parfaits. These make a decadent dessert, as well as a fun breakfast. Serve these in early summer when berries are in season.

Mixed-Berry Cream Parfaits

¾ **cup fresh blueberries**

¾ **cup fresh blackberries**

¾ **cup fresh raspberries**

2 **cups creamy vanilla or creamy strawberry low-fat yogurt**

2 **roasted almond crunchy granola bars (1 pouch from 8.9-oz box)**

1 Divide berries among 4 parfait glasses or dessert dishes. Top each with ½ cup yogurt.

2 While granola bars are still in the pouch, break into coarse pieces with hands. Sprinkle granola pieces over fruit and yogurt. Serve immediately.

1 Serving: Calories 190; Total Fat 3g (Saturated Fat 1g, Trans Fat 0g); Cholesterol 0mg; Sodium 105mg; Total Carbohydrate 36g (Dietary Fiber 4g); Protein 5g **Exchanges:** 1 Fruit, 1 Other Carbohydrate, ½ Skim Milk, ½ Fat **Carbohydrate Choices:** 2½

This delightful fruit dessert will thrill kids and adults alike with its flower-like presentation. Try to get fresh strawberries in season (May and June in many regions); the flavor is sweet and the texture is heavenly.

Prep Time:
20 Minutes

Start to Finish:
20 Minutes

12 servings

Strawberry Blossoms

12	large fresh strawberries	2	tablespoons powdered sugar
3	oz (from 8-oz package) cream cheese, softened	1	tablespoon sour cream
			Small fresh mint leaves, if desired

1. Remove stems from strawberries to form a flat base. Place strawberries, pointed ends up, on cutting board. With sharp knife, carefully slice each strawberry in half vertically to within ¼ inch of base. Cut each half into 3 wedges to form 6 petals (do not slice through base). Carefully pull petals apart slightly.

2. In small bowl, beat cream cheese, powdered sugar and sour cream until light and fluffy. Spoon mixture into strawberries. (Or spoon mixture into decorating bag fitted with star tip and pipe into berries.) Garnish with mint.

1 Serving: Calories 40; Total Fat 2.5g (Saturated Fat 1.5g, Trans Fat 0g); Cholesterol 10mg; Sodium 25mg; Total Carbohydrate 3g (Dietary Fiber 0g); Protein 0g **Exchanges:** ½ Fat **Carbohydrate Choices:** 0

> TRY THIS Try strawberry-flavored or any other sweet-flavored cream cheese instead of plain cream cheese.

Use store-bought cookies to make this crazy-fast, kid-pleasing dessert with yogurt and the lemony zip of citrus zest.

Prep Time:
5 Minutes

Start to Finish:
5 Minutes

1 serving

Lemon Meringue Pie Bowl

1	container (6 oz) lemon burst low-fat yogurt	2	meringue cookies
		1	teaspoon grated lemon peel

1 Spoon yogurt into small dessert bowl. Top with cookies. Sprinkle with lemon peel.

1 Serving: Calories 140; Total Fat 0g (Saturated Fat 0g, Trans Fat 0g); Cholesterol 0mg; Sodium 95mg; Total Carbohydrate 30g (Dietary Fiber 0g); Protein 5g **Exchanges:** 1½ Other Carbohydrate, ½ Skim Milk **Carbohydrate Choices:** 2

15
MINUTES
OR LESS

Treat your family to a quick and easy dessert that features both raspberries and raspberry yogurt for an extra fruity treat.

Prep Time:
15 Minutes

Start to Finish:
15 Minutes

8 servings

Raspberry Yogurt Celebration Dessert

1   **bag (10 oz) frozen raspberries (without syrup), thawed**

2   **cups frozen (thawed) fat-free whipped topping**

2   **containers (6 oz each) red raspberry fat-free yogurt**

1   **package (5 oz) meringue cookies, crumbled**

Fresh mint leaves, if desired

1   Place raspberries in blender. Cover; blend on high speed until smooth. Set puree aside.

2   In large bowl, mix whipped topping and yogurt. Fold in crumbled cookies and half of the raspberry puree. Spoon into 1 large chilled serving bowl or 8 individual chilled bowls; drizzle with remaining raspberry puree. Garnish with mint.

1 Serving: Calories 140; Total Fat 0.5g (Saturated Fat 0g, Trans Fat 0g); Cholesterol 0mg; Sodium 40mg; Total Carbohydrate 30g (Dietary Fiber 2g); Protein 2g **Exchanges:** ½ Starch, 1½ Other Carbohydrate **Carbohydrate Choices:** 2

Grilling intensifies the flavor of fruit, and stone fruit like peaches especially benefit from the heat of the grill. Serve with ice cream or sweetened cream for an extra-fun treat.

Prep Time:
25 Minutes

Start to Finish:
25 Minutes

4 servings

Streusel-Topped Grilled Peaches

STREUSEL

2 tablespoons all-purpose flour

1 tablespoon packed brown sugar

1 tablespoon cold butter

PEACHES

1½ teaspoons granulated sugar

⅛ teaspoon ground cinnamon

⅛ teaspoon ground ginger

   Vegetable oil

2 large ripe peaches or nectarines, pitted, cut in half

1 tablespoon butter, melted

1 Heat gas or charcoal grill. In small bowl, mix flour and brown sugar. Cut in cold butter with fork until mixture looks like dry bread crumbs (use fingers if necessary); set aside. Cut 18x8-inch sheet of heavy-duty foil; bring up foil to form sides. Spread streusel mixture evenly in foil; set aside. In small bowl, mix granulated sugar, cinnamon and ginger; set aside.

2 Carefully brush one side of grill rack with vegetable oil. Place peaches, cut sides down, on oiled side of grill. Place foil container with streusel on other side of grill. Cook peaches over medium heat 3 minutes. Cook streusel 3 to 6 minutes or until light golden brown, stirring frequently with long-handled spoon. Remove foil with streusel from grill; set aside.

3 After 3 minutes, turn peaches cut sides up. Brush cut sides with melted butter; sprinkle with sugar mixture. Cook about 3 minutes longer or until softened. Turn peaches cut sides down; cook 1 to 2 minutes or until cut sides are caramelized. To serve, sprinkle peach halves evenly with streusel.

1 Serving: Calories 120; Total Fat 6g (Saturated Fat 3.5g, Trans Fat 0g); Cholesterol 15mg; Sodium 50mg; Total Carbohydrate 16g (Dietary Fiber 1g); Protein 1g **Exchanges:** ½ Starch, ½ Fruit, 1 Fat **Carbohydrate Choices:** 1

A yummy batter, apples and cinnamon bake up to make impossibly delicious little "apple pies" topped with whipped cream, caramel, pecans and sea salt. You won't miss the traditional pie crust!

Prep Time:
10 Minutes

Start to Finish:
30 Minutes

12 mini pies

Impossibly Easy Salted Caramel Apple Mini Pies

FILLING

- 1½ **cups diced peeled Granny Smith apples**
- ¾ **teaspoon ground cinnamon**
- ⅛ **teaspoon ground nutmeg**

BATTER

- ½ **cup Original Bisquick mix**
- ⅓ **cup sugar**
- ⅓ **cup milk**
- 2 **tablespoons butter, melted**
- 1 **egg**

TOPPING

- ¾ **cup sweetened whipped cream**
- ½ **cup caramel topping**
- ¼ **cup chopped pecans, toasted**
  Coarse sea salt

1 Heat oven to 375°F. Place paper baking cup in each of 12 regular-size muffin cups; spray cups with cooking spray.

2 In small bowl, mix filling ingredients; set aside.

3 In another small bowl, stir batter ingredients with whisk or fork until blended. Spoon 1 level measuring tablespoon of batter into each muffin cup. Top with 2 measuring tablespoons of apple mixture. Spoon 1 level measuring tablespoon of batter over apples in each muffin cup.

4 Bake 15 minutes or until set in center and edges are golden brown. Cool 5 minutes; remove from pan to cooling rack. To serve, remove paper baking cups. Place each pie on dessert plate or in small bowl; top with 1 tablespoon whipped cream, 2 teaspoons caramel topping, 1 teaspoon pecans and a sprinkle of salt.

1 Mini Pie: Calories 140; Total Fat 6g (Saturated Fat 2.5g, Trans Fat 0g); Cholesterol 25mg; Sodium 140mg; Total Carbohydrate 21g (Dietary Fiber 0g); Protein 1g **Exchanges:** ½ Starch, 1 Other Carbohydrate, 1 Fat **Carbohydrate Choices:** 1½

Short on time but want to serve a traditional dessert? Check out this mouth-watering cobbler packed with fresh berries—a delicious treat. Serve with ice cream or whipped cream, if you like.

Prep Time:
10 Minutes

Start to Finish:
30 Minutes

6 servings

Fresh Berry Cobbler

½	cup sugar	1	cup Original Bisquick mix
1	tablespoon cornstarch	¼	cup milk
4	cups fresh raspberries or blueberries	1	tablespoon sugar
2	tablespoons water	1	tablespoon butter, melted
1	teaspoon lemon juice		

1 Heat oven to 425°F. In 2-quart saucepan, mix ½ cup sugar and the cornstarch. Stir in berries, water and lemon juice. Heat to boiling over medium heat, stirring constantly. Boil and stir 1 minute. Pour mixture into ungreased 8- or 9-inch round (1½- or 2-quart) glass baking dish.

2 In medium bowl, stir Bisquick mix, milk, 1 tablespoon sugar and the melted butter just until blended and dough forms. Drop dough by 6 spoonfuls onto hot berry mixture.

3 Bake about 15 minutes or until filling is bubbly and topping is light brown. Cool about 5 minutes. Serve warm with whipped cream.

1 Serving: Calories 205; Total Fat 5g (Saturated Fat 1g, Trans Fat 0g); Cholesterol 0mg; Sodium 310mg; Total Carbohydrate 39g (Dietary Fiber 1g); Protein 2g **Exchanges:** 1 Starch, ½ Fruit, 1 Other Carbohydrate, 1 Fat **Carbohydrate Choices:** 2½

> TRY THIS Pass a pitcher of whipping cream, half-and-half or eggnog, when it's available, to pour over bowls of warm cobbler. Sprinkle a little ground cinnamon or nutmeg on top for just a hint of spiciness.

Take dessert over the top with a ramped-up banana split. Dulce de leche tops two kinds of ice cream for a memorable and decadent meal-ender.

Dulce de Leche Banana Splits

1   can (13.4 oz) dulce de leche (caramelized sweetened condensed milk)

3   to 4 tablespoons milk

2   medium bananas

4   small scoops (¼ cup each) vanilla ice cream

4   small scoops (¼ cup each) chocolate ice cream

1   cup whipped cream topping (from aerosol can)

½   cup chopped salted dry-roasted peanuts

4   maraschino cherries with stems

1   In small bowl, stir dulce de leche and enough milk with whisk to make a smooth, pourable sauce.

2   Cut each banana in half lengthwise and then crosswise. In each of 4 stemmed dessert glasses or bowls, place 2 banana quarters along outer edges. Top each with 1 scoop vanilla ice cream and 1 scoop chocolate ice cream. Spoon dulce de leche mixture evenly over ice cream. Top with whipped cream, peanuts and cherries. Serve immediately.

1 Serving: Calories 690; Total Fat 25g (Saturated Fat 12g, Trans Fat 0g); Cholesterol 45mg; Sodium 280mg; Total Carbohydrate 100g (Dietary Fiber 4g); Protein 13g **Exchanges:** 1 Starch, ½ Fruit, 5 Other Carbohydrate, 1½ High-Fat Meat, 2½ Fat **Carbohydrate Choices:** 6½

> TIME-SAVER To assemble these banana splits even faster, scoop the ice cream onto a tray ahead of time; cover and store in the freezer until ready to serve.

A fast spin on a fancy dessert, this version is prepared in just 10 minutes in the microwave. For best texture and flavor, use medium-ripe bananas.

Prep Time:
10 Minutes

Start to Finish:
10 Minutes

4 servings

Bananas Foster with Ice Cream

½	cup fat-free caramel topping	2	bananas, cut into chunks
2	teaspoons dark rum or 1 teaspoon rum extract	2	cups vanilla low-fat ice cream

1 In small microwavable bowl, mix caramel topping and rum. Microwave uncovered on High 30 seconds or until very warm. Stir in bananas.

2 Scoop ice cream onto dessert dishes; top with banana mixture.

1 Serving: Calories 29; Total Fat 3g (Saturated Fat 2g, Trans Fat 0g); Cholesterol 20mg; Sodium 200mg; Total Carbohydrate 60g (Dietary Fiber 2g); Protein 5g **Exchanges:** 1 Fruit, 2½ Other Carbohydrate, ½ Low-Fat Milk, ½ Fat **Carbohydrate Choices:** 4

Prep Time:
10 Minutes

Start to Finish:
10 Minutes

4 servings

Orange juice concentrate makes a great sweetener, as in this sundae-like concoction with sweetened yogurt, fresh fruit and a decadent chocolate drizzle.

Chocolate-Laced Kiwifruit with Orange Sauce

½ cup plain fat-free yogurt

1 tablespoon frozen (partially thawed) orange juice concentrate

4 large kiwifruit, peeled, cut into ¼-inch slices

2 tablespoons dark or semisweet chocolate chips

1 teaspoon vegetable oil

1 In small bowl, mix yogurt and orange juice concentrate; spoon 2 tablespoons onto each of 4 dessert plates. Arrange kiwifruit on yogurt mixture.

2 In 1-cup microwavable measuring cup, microwave chocolate chips and oil uncovered on High 30 to 60 seconds, stirring every 15 seconds, until melted and smooth. Carefully drizzle chocolate in thin lines over kiwifruit.

1 Serving: Calories 110; Total Fat 3g (Saturated Fat 1g, Trans Fat 0g); Cholesterol 0mg; Sodium 25mg; Total Carbohydrate 17g (Dietary Fiber 2g); Protein 2g **Exchanges:** ½ Starch, ½ Fruit, ½ Fat **Carbohydrate Choices:** 1

Few desserts say "comfort food" like baked apples. The microwave speeds up prep so that you can dig into these caramel-topped treats sooner.

Prep Time:
5 Minutes

Start to Finish:
15 Minutes

2 servings

Baked Apples with Rum-Caramel Sauce

2 small baking apples	**1** tablespoon caramel topping
1 tablespoon water	**2** teaspoons rum or apple cider
½ cup vanilla reduced-fat ice cream	**Dash** ground cinnamon

1 Cut thin slice off bottom and top of each apple. Using paring knife or apple corer, remove core from each apple.

2 In 8- or 9-inch square microwavable dish, place apples upright. Pour 1 tablespoon water over apples; cover. Microwave on High 8 to 10 minutes or until apples are tender.

3 Place apples in dessert bowls; reserve 1 teaspoon cooking liquid. Cut each apple in half. Spoon ¼ cup ice cream between apple halves. In small bowl, stir caramel topping, rum and 1 teaspoon reserved cooking liquid; pour over apples. Sprinkle with cinnamon.

1 Serving: Calories 200; Total Fat 1g (Saturated Fat 0g, Trans Fat 0g); Cholesterol 0mg; Sodium 110mg; Total Carbohydrate 44g (Dietary Fiber 5g); Protein 2g **Exchanges:** ½ Starch, 2½ Other Carbohydrate **Carbohydrate Choices:** 3

> TRY THIS Omit the ice cream and instead top the apples with a crunchy granola bar, crushed, and a dollop of frozen (thawed) fat-free whipped topping.

15 MINUTES OR LESS

Prep Time:
10 Minutes

Start to Finish:
15 Minutes

1 serving

Dessert for one is easy and varied with a mug and a microwave. Choose fruit based on what you're craving or what's in season, then build a great cobbler just for you.

Build-Your-Own Microwave Mug Cobbler

½	cup fresh fruit (such as blueberries, strawberries, peaches), chopped if necessary
2	tablespoons sugar
¼	cup Original Bisquick mix
⅛	teaspoon ground cinnamon, if desired
½	teaspoon grated lemon or orange peel, if desired
1	tablespoon chopped nuts (pecans, almonds or walnuts), if desired
1	tablespoon old-fashioned oats, if desired
1	tablespoon milk

1 In microwavable mug*, mix fruit and 1 tablespoon of the sugar.

2 In small bowl, stir Bisquick mix, remaining 1 tablespoon sugar, and any of the "if desired" ingredients. Add milk; stir until thick dough forms. Drop dough in clumps over fruit in mug. Sprinkle dough with coarse sugar, if desired.

3 Microwave uncovered on High 1 minute 30 seconds to 2 minutes or until fruit bubbles to top of mug. Cobbler will be very hot; wait 5 minutes before serving. Top with whipped cream or ice cream, if desired.

*Do not fill your mug more than two-thirds full or it will bubble over. You may need to adjust the recipe slightly to fit your mug. For easy cleanup, place mug on microwavable plate in microwave to catch any juices that bubble over.

1 Serving: Calories 290; Total Fat 5g (Saturated Fat 1.5g, Trans Fat 0.5g); Cholesterol 0mg; Sodium 380mg; Total Carbohydrate 57g (Dietary Fiber 2g); Protein 3g **Exchanges:** 1 Starch, ½ Fruit, 2½ Other Carbohydrate, 1 Fat **Carbohydrate Choices:** 4

Metric Conversion Guide

Volume

U.S. Units	Canadian Metric	Australian Metric
¼ teaspoon	1 mL	1 ml
½ teaspoon	2 mL	2 ml
1 teaspoon	5 mL	5 ml
1 tablespoon	15 mL	20 ml
¼ cup	50 mL	60 ml
⅓ cup	75 mL	80 ml
½ cup	125 mL	125 ml
⅔ cup	150 mL	170 ml
¾ cup	175 mL	190 ml
1 cup	250 mL	250 ml
1 quart	1 liter	1 liter
1½ quarts	1.5 liters	1.5 liters
2 quarts	2 liters	2 liters
2½ quarts	2.5 liters	2.5 liters
3 quarts	3 liters	3 liters
4 quarts	4 liters	4 liters

Weight

U.S. Units	Canadian Metric	Australian Metric
1 ounce	30 grams	30 grams
2 ounces	55 grams	60 grams
3 ounces	85 grams	90 grams
4 ounces (¼ pound)	115 grams	125 grams
8 ounces (½ pound)	225 grams	225 grams
16 ounces (1 pound)	455 grams	500 grams
1 pound	455 grams	0.5 kilogram

Measurements

Inches	Centimeters
1	2.5
2	5.0
3	7.5
4	10.0
5	12.5
6	15.0
7	17.5
8	20.5
9	23.0
10	25.5
11	28.0
12	30.5
13	33.0

Temperatures

Fahrenheit	Celsius
32°	0°
212°	100°
250°	120°
275°	140°
300°	150°
325°	160°
350°	180°
375°	190°
400°	200°
425°	220°
450°	230°
475°	240°
500°	260°

Note: The recipes in this cookbook have not been developed or tested using metric measures. When converting recipes to metric, some variations in quality may be noted.

Index

RECIPE TESTING AND CALCULATING NUTRITION INFORMATION

RECIPE TESTING:

- Large eggs and 2% milk were used unless otherwise indicated.

- Fat-free, low-fat, low-sodium or lite products were not used unless indicated.

- No nonstick cookware and bakeware were used unless otherwise indicated. No dark-colored, black or insulated bakeware was used.

- When a pan is specified, a metal pan was used; a baking dish or pie plate means ovenproof glass was used.

- An electric hand mixer was used for mixing only when mixer speeds are specified.

CALCULATING NUTRITION:

- The first ingredient was used wherever a choice is given, such as ⅓ cup sour cream or plain yogurt.

- The first amount was used wherever a range is given, such as 3- to 3½-pound whole chicken.

- The first serving number was used wherever a range is given, such as 4 to 6 servings.

- "If desired" ingredients were not included.

- Only the amount of a marinade or frying oil that is absorbed was included.